MW00584022

"The residents of Point Pleasant enjoy reading the short stories and poems written by Dick Smith. These frequently appear in our monthly newsletter the 'ECHO.' Like his previous books, Dick Smith demonstrates his positive philosophy towards life and growing old. His humor, his observations and his ability to deal with loneliness, grief, stress and aging are admirable. He continues to live, to love and to enjoy life!"

—MEDA RIGATTI, author of *Memories & Stories from an Italian Nonna*

"Congratulations to Dr. Richard Smith, PhD, for his scintillating, discerning, and remarkably penned collection of prose and poetry. Dr. Smith, better known as Dick, has taken the reader on a journey from witticism to heartbreak. His stories and poems carry the reader through every emotion with a sensitivity that draws long-buried memories to the forefront. Dick's talent for tenderly touching our humanity is rare. It is a pleasure to read *Tales from a Twilight House* with its deep insights into the lives of the elderly."

—CARY LETSCHE

"*Tales from a Twilight House* provides a front row seat to the joys and sorrows, daily struggles and personal insights of a resident who navigates through life in a retirement community. Dick Smith's commentary is so poignant and relevant that I have often used excerpts for our chapel services and leadership devotionals. As the chaplain of his retirement community, I can only say that his words have deeply impacted me and my ministry to our residents."

—DINO SILVESTRINI

"The author of this book is 89 years old, and he is high on life. People, places and things, in his past and in his present, make him happy. Sometimes he needs to inject a shot of humor, or engage in some deep thinking, to find the happy, but page after page this book gets there. If you wish you could love life more, pick up this book, and it will take your hand, and lead the way."

—SUZANNE LAURION

"The author is reflecting on life in the 'twilight years,' those years before our passage from this life. But that's not all he's doing. Dick Smith also puts us in touch with the impact of WWII on lives in small towns and with the cultural and technological changes over the years. His reflections on life include insights from greats like Shakespeare and Browning to the low-wage laborer at the neighborhood bar on Friday night. We see life from the Gold Star mother whose son didn't return from battle as well as the hopeful child waiting for Christmas. Smith is at once a psychologist, philosopher and sociologist. To round out his stories and reflections, this 'musing old man' has interspersed poetry, some contemplative and some filled with a playful humor not unlike that found in Dr. Seuss. I loved this book and look forward to sharing it with friends and family of all ages. I guarantee you will like it too, whatever your age."

—DR. SUSAN R. MOORE

"Knowing this author for 5 years, I was more than ready to take one more Dick Smith excursion by reading an early draft of his upcoming *Tales from a Twilight House*. For me, this time, it became easy to jump aboard and enjoy the ride upon the graceful broad wings of one of my favorite authors, neighbors and friends.

"What a pleasure to soar the blue skies together in the latter stage of Dick's long, fruitful and productive life. We joined in flight, dipping into his sunny happy thoughts, clear observations of life and people; occasionally encountering a few rough winds tossing author and reader through traumatic times. I felt exhilarated as he guided me through sunshine, clouds and moments of rain—as he experienced a full life of 90 years that is still gracefully ongoing.

"I am always enchanted by Dick's down-home style, mid-western sensibility when reciting anecdotes, perceptive observations and offering lessons—all free for my taking. He forever impresses me by his readiness to expose his own sensitive and romantic feelings through prose and poetry. I guess I am a pushover for Dick's completeness: his writing exhibits the strength of a man balanced by a warm, affectionate feminine nature.

"IF I had similar experiences in my 75 years, what he relates in personal details of his own longer life's journey helps me cherish, appreciate and translate into fond memories my own. IF I never enjoyed some of his experiences myself—idyllic family gatherings, interactions with children, or educator career—he captivates me in a manner that his details become my own."

— CAROL LEE GILBERT

"A spirited narrative of one man's understanding and acceptance of old age, captured in prose and poetry. Through his writings the author takes us on a journey through his twilight years, remembering the people, places and events that create the mosaic of a life well lived."

—JOHN S. GENDRON, Mesa Arizona

Tales from a Twilight House

by Richard J. Smith, Ph.D.

© Copyright 2020 Richard J. Smith, Ph.D.

ISBN 978-1-64663-006-6

All rights reserved. No part of this publication may be reproduced, stored in a retrieval system, or transmitted in any form or by any means—electronic, mechanical, photocopy, recording, or any other—except for brief quotations in printed reviews, without the prior written permission of the author.

Published by

 köehlerbooks™

210 60th Street
Virginia Beach, VA 23451
800-435-4811
www.koehlerbooks.com

TALES

—— *from a* ——

TWILIGHT
HOUSE

RICHARD J. SMITH, PH.D.

VIRGINIA BEACH
CAPE CHARLES

TABLE *of* CONTENTS

FOREWORD

You are about to embark on one man's journey through old age. *Tales From a Twilight House* is a compilation of his thoughts, realizations, and his acknowledgement of old age. He tells how people in their twilight years come to know and accept the end of life.

Some of Dr. Richard Smith's essays, stories and poems in *Tales* have appeared in our retirement community's publications—our newspaper the *ECHO*, and the *WRITER'S QUARTERLY*, which provides an outlet for creative writing. These publications play a significant role in the life of retirement communities and are produced by the residents and written by and for them.

Residents enjoy articles written by neighbors and look forward to what their favorite columnist has to say. As the former editor of the *ECHO* and the present editor of the *WRITER'S QUARTERLY*, I have had the pleasure of working with many contributors to our publications, and one of our most popular and prolific contributors is Dr. Smith.

As soon as the Smiths moved into Westminster Point Pleasant in Bradenton, Florida, he began writing about his new life in a retirement community. He says he discovered a completely different world—a new culture—from any he had ever inhabited.

And, he liked to write about this new culture he had moved into. He wrote about the people here, residents and staff, he wrote about the organization; and he wrote about how he felt about being part of this community. Residents look forward to reading his thought-provoking, and entertaining essays and poems.

The way residents and staff responded to his writing inspired him to write this, and three other books since moving here in 2013.

A well-known author of many college text books and professional journal articles, Dr. Smith's non-technical books are thoughtful, delightful and a most rewarding read!

CAROLE SANDERS, EDITOR
WRITER'S QUARTERLY

To the residents of all twilight houses who have chosen to live their old ages in comfort and joy with other old folks.

PREFACE

There is not much I remember about my elementary school years with the School Sisters of Notre Dame in charge. But I do remember my third–grade teacher, Sister Germaine. She gave me my start as a writer by assigning a Christmas poem writing contest. I won the contest, and Sister Germaine had me come to the front of the class and read it to all the losers.

Every Monday we were given a list of words we were to learn how to spell. We were tested on them every Friday afternoon. I was good at spelling and may have been the only third grader who could correctly spell *lackadaisical* correctly on the first try.

Because she gave me my start as a writer, I owe a lot to Sister Germaine. I use the words on her spelling-words lists as often as I can to pay her back. However, write as much as I have—and I have written almost as much as Charles Dickens—I have never found a good sentence for *lackadaisical*.

So, Sister Germaine, wherever you are, I have just done it. Now with that debt paid, let me introduce you to the book you are about to read. It contains a collection of poems and essays written from the perspective of an old man. It's not true that old age is all in your head—well, maybe some of it is:

> *"I forgot."*
> *I say that more and more.*
> *As my memory loses its sharpness.*
> *"Where did I put that?"*
> *"Sorry I missed that appointment."*
> *"Why was I going to call my doctor?"*
> *"What channel is ESPN?"*
> *"Why did I come in here?"*
> *"Which drawer is it in?"*
> *"I'll never forget old—What's his name?"*
> *Sometimes I stop mid-sentence.*
> *Names and faces don't always connect.*
> *Just as I have had to downsize my life.*
> *My memory has downsized too.*

I'm not there yet, but many of those in their eighties are. In this book you will be offered a better understanding of us old folks.

One of the persons I spoke with while gathering material for an earlier book, equated old age with any other age in life. "There's good and bad no matter how old you are," he said. I don't agree. I have found all definable ages to be different.

Old age is especially different because it is the *final* age. In some characteristics we resemble children. We need others to be patient with us, to care for us, and to help us grow, but not toward more independence and strength. Rather, we need to be helped to grow toward increasing weakness and dependence.

Old age is a time of richness and poverty. A time of liberation and entrapment. To assert that old age is what you make of it is an oversimplification. Old age is often in control.

Old age is the least understood of all the ages. We can't hear from those who have lived it. At this writing, I'm eighty-nine and can firmly attest that there aren't many born in 1930 writing about it. So, bear with me as this older man gives it another try.

Three years ago, I published a book similar to this one under the title, *Musings of an Old Man*. It was well received by readers. A friend suggested I write another and title it *Musings of an Older Man*. I opted instead to title this one, *Tales from a Twilight House* because I am deeply in the twilight of my life. I write this book because I have been so richly rewarded by others I have written. *Musings* reached people in ways I never imagined.

So, how does it happen that a man who has outlived his life expectancy by a decade or more is still writing? Perhaps it's because I take time each day to ponder the passing scene. I wonder what my four children, my nine grandchildren and my eight—and still counting—great grandchildren have in store for them as the seasons pass and they find themselves passing time by musing as I have. And I wonder why I am so fortunate as to have a loving family, many friends, a good place to live, and a good friend who is also a good editor who isn't shy about saying, "You can do better than this." And I wonder what God has in store for me when I close my eyes for the last time, as I watched my beloved wife of sixty-three years do four years earlier. I often mouth the words of an old song, *"What's it all about, Alfie?"*

I don't have nearly as much before me as I have left behind. The entrance door is much farther from me than the exit door. I can now feel myself growing older as I could not when I was younger. I accept that because I can't change it. I may stay alive and active, but my threshold for activity is decreasing.

Now I find myself contemplating what life is all about, attempting to describe it as I have lived it. I have been poor, and I have been rich. I have been happy, and I have been sad. I have been on hills, and I have been in valleys. So how do I sum up all that I have experienced in eighty-nine years?

It seems to me that life is an escalating process of saying goodbye. I have left a lot behind me. I have said goodbye to youth, middle age, a mother, a father, a brother, even a wife. I have said goodbye to friends and material possessions of all kinds: cars, jobs, clothing, homes.

Every morning I read the obituaries from four different papers.
Places I've lived. I remember those places well.
Today I brought to screen an obit that made me sad.
Fred Wilty dies. We called him "Fritz."
And my list of former friends is shorter by one.
One by one, I am losing my old friends.
I have downsized a lot of my life.
My lawnmower and bicycle are long gone.
And now I am downsizing my friends.
The news of their passing comes now from pages I don't turn.

A few right clicks and Fritz is in the news on the screen.
I know Fritz would be pleased I got the news, he wouldn't care how.
He would be especially pleased the news brought
His old friend good memories.
Memories of the days Fritz and I delivered the news
Of the day on our bicycles,
And our customers turned to Page 3 to read about who died that day.

But new doors have always opened. The former has always been replaced by a new present, sometimes better than the old.

Soon I will say my final goodbye. I must have faith and hope that a hand will open another door and I will be sustained behind that final door as I have been sustained behind preceding doors. All our lives hands open doors for us.

A parent takes the hand of a child learning to walk.
A hand is offered to a grieving friend.
A stranger takes the hand of an older pedestrian to cross a street.
Let me shake your hand for all you have done for me.
I give you my hand in love.

We shake hands, we hold hands with someone we love, we wave, we give high-fives. Our hands applaud, offer sympathy, greet others, are folded in prayer and anoint the dying. They express our humanity, our empathy with one another, our fidelity to our God. "Take my hand." Three beautiful words. When I am in need of comfort, appreciation, guidance, friendship, love, I want someone to say, "Take my hand." When I see someone who needs a hand I will offer mine. And when I die, I hope I hear God say, "Take my hand."

Every day I am thankful for what I have left after eighty-nine years of wear and tear on this body and spirit. That causes me to wonder why God has given others so much less? I live in a retirement community where the average age of the residents is eighty-three. Some are managing their final years nicely; others are not. I write for them all. I am told they look forward to reading what I write for them in our monthly publication. That pleases me and gives me purpose. In this book I offer you what I write for them, some prose and poetry to ponder. Some is joyful, some sad. God has equipped us with both laughter and tears. Life requires us to use both.

Everybody should have a pleasant-memory spot, a time or place when we felt safe, loved, at peace. I have some, and they are always there when I need them. When I am, as Shakespeare wrote "in disgrace with fortune and men's eyes, when I all alone . . . beweep my outcast state."

Don't we all have moments when we need to remind ourselves that life was once good and will be again, that this down-time is temporary? Tears can be dried. "Every cloud has a silver lining." Remember that one?

Life is filled with peaks and valleys. "Wait until the sun shines through." Haven't we all felt desperate at some time or another, sure we will never be right again, until the sun comes up and we can see our clouds disappearing? Then our load lightens.

When I find myself in an unpleasant time or space, I am reminded that life was good—and will be again.

Yesterday a sweet memory came and went.
I couldn't catch it, hold it, make it stay awhile.
It was a momentary illumination,
Bright and beautiful.
Enough to taste, but not to swallow.
For a second I was there again,
Just for a fast remembrance.
Long enough for me to smile.

And know there once was a place and time I swam in happiness.

I.

GOOD OL' DAYS

O nce in a while, I treat myself to a childhood memory. And like so many lodged in our brains, we tend to romanticize them. My recollections are just that.

I grew up in Marinette, Wisconsin, fifty miles north of Green Bay. The winter temperature often registered below zero. Coughs, sneezes and runny noses were part of my life in the winter. The sleeve of every boy's mackinaw was crusty from nose wiping. Nobody paid attention until you ran a fever. Then you stayed home from school until your temperature registered normal.

Running a fever was a blessing—no school, and you could stay in your pajamas all day. However, in the evening body temperatures begin to rise, and being sick stopped being fun. Then mama tucked you into bed.

Now tucking into bed in the winter was something that had to be done with precision. We wore flannel pajamas, and the bed sheets were also flannel. Wherever you landed was where you stuck. So Mama positioned you on your back, near the edge of the bed where you would be easy to reach. Then she rubbed your chest with Vicks VapoRub. I can remember that feeling and that smell to this day. Finally, she safety-pinned a flannel cloth around your neck, jabbed a finger of Vicks VapoRub up both nostrils and kissed you good night.

In a day or two you were well enough and eager to go back to school, smelling strongly, of Vick's VapoRub, just like all the kids who returned to school after their fevers were gone.

As I think back on it, I'm so glad Florida is warm. I much prefer the smell of sunscreen to VapoRub. But childhood memories of Wisconsin still warm me.

When you drove up to a pump at a gas station in the good old days, an attendant in uniform came out, pumped the gas you ordered, cleaned your windows, checked the air in your tires, filled them if they were low, checked your oil level, added oil if needed and even added water to your battery, if needed. Gasoline was twenty-five cents a gallon. Beer was ten cents a glass, you were not expected to tip the bartender, and I made sixty-five cents an hour working my way through college.

Our bigger cities were much smaller when I was growing up, and they were more connected to the rural areas. Many of the "city-slickers" had begun life on a farm and had friends and relatives who were still farmers. Farms were small. Forty-acre farms were more prevalent than *eighties*.

To accommodate farmers, stores in the small towns originally remained open until nine o'clock Saturday nights. But some of the farmers partied in the taverns after the stores closed and missed church on Sundays. So, the town clergymen petitioned the stores to stay open Friday nights instead. The store owners complied, and that gave rise to the Friday night tavern fish fry to get the business of the Catholic farmers who couldn't eat meat on Fridays.

Most farmers and many city folks didn't have telephones, so friends and relatives of farmers were always prepared for Friday night drop-ins. The farmers brought fresh-picked produce or canned foods for a gift, in addition to conversation, and their hosts offered a drink and dessert in return.

Farmers and their city cousins often got together at the dance hall to celebrate Saturday nights, holidays, weddings, showers and big-family reunions. And most families were big in those days. Our dance hall was several miles beyond the city limits and was called the Blue Ribbon.

It was just a big hall with a bar, a bandstand, several long tables and benches along the walls. Locally brewed beer was on tap, and the tables had food when showers, weddings or reunions were held there. Cheese, sausage, homemade breads, crackers, pickles, salads, deviled eggs, pies, cookies and cakes, provided by the hosts, were heaped on the tables. Farmers worked hard and partied hard. If the social events were held in the afternoon and evenings, someone in the family left to milk the cows and feed the animals and returned to dance the night away.

Dancing was big in those days, mostly waltzes and polkas. The music was usually provided by local musicians. Often a piano, fiddle, drum, accordion and a tuba made the music. Most polkas ended with a *WHUMP* or two from the tuba.

Grandmas and grandpas danced with toddlers. No woman could refuse a dance with a man who was sober. Men danced more with other women than with their wives, except for the first and last dance. (I forgot that once, but my wife never did.) Young lovers danced belly to belly and cheek to cheek and called for slow music. Teenage boys snickered on the sidelines at the teenage girls dancing with each other. Sometimes, on a dare, a boy asked a girl to dance or a girl asked a boy. Some of the older boys sneaked out to the parking lot for a nip of whiskey from a bottle they had stashed in the trunk.

The first supermarket I remember was the A and P (Atlantic & Pacific Tea Company). A common joke was, "Let's go to the A and P." Soon after the A and P had plenty of competition with supermarkets names that didn't give rise to jokes.

Prior to supermarkets people either grew, baked, butchered their food and/or went to the corner grocery store. Every neighborhood had one.

The owner ran the store solo or with the help of a spouse and perhaps children on Saturdays and school vacations. No stores were open Sundays back then. The grocer helped unload the delivery trucks, shelved the items and served the customers, usually wearing an apron. Some stores had shelves that could be reached only with a ladder. Typically, the shopper presented the grocer with a list of items. Then the grocer scurried about collecting what was ordered and bagging it. Most regulars brought a cloth bag to carry the items home, on foot or on a bicycle. Cars were rarely used to go to the corner grocery.

The item for sale we old-timers remember best is the penny candy. Every grocery store had a glass case filled with a variety of candies—a penny each. Licorice whips, candy cigarettes, hard candy, soda pop in little wax bottles were favorites. When a stay-at-home mother wanted to get rid of the kids for a while, she gave them each a penny and lay down for a nap. The older kids took the little ones by the hand, walked them to the store and helped them select a penny candy.

Other than the penny candy the stores sold bread, cookies, canned goods of all kinds, salt, pepper, sandwich meat and sometimes pork chops, cubed steak or hamburger, depending on the refrigeration, which was scarce in those days. Most homes and stores had iceboxes filled with blocks of ice delivered by *icemen* in the *ice truck*.

Our corner grocery store sold groceries on credit. I remember going to the store with my parents every weekly payday. They did their shopping and paid their bill. On payday the grocer always gave me a cookie or let me choose a few penny candies. He must have been in a good mood one payday. He gave me a nickel box of Cracker Jax, with a toy inside every box.

Stores and taverns closed on Sundays so all people could go to church and spend the day with their families. While Sunday church was not required, people who went to no church were looked upon suspiciously. People married younger than they do today, and something other than a church marriage was rare. Large families were the norm.

My small town of 12,000 had four Catholic parishes (French, German, Polish and Irish). Each had its own eight-grade elementary school staffed by nuns. Now there is one parish with lay teachers. Protestant ministers tell me their parish populations are declining also. They cite a growing absence of young congregants.

Religion played a bigger role in the family lives of people then than it does now.

One characteristic of life in the old days that may have made them *gooder* was the sense of self-determination. There was more of the world to be developed and fewer people to develop that world. Young people had more choices, more roads that led to the good life. Anyone who wanted a college education was able to get one. State colleges were inexpensive. I paid something like two-hundred dollars a semester, and I could rent my textbooks for a few dollars more. The state picked up the rest. I worked my way through a state teacher's college making sixty-five cents an hour and $600 in summer jobs.

Of course, these good times occurred after the thirties, when almost everyone was out of work and poor because of the Great Depression. President Franklin Delano Roosevelt began to turn the economy around with his government-funded programs that paid the unemployed to work repairing and improving the country's infrastructure.

Then World War II came along, and the farm boys and some girls and the city boys and some girls went off to war.

★ ☆ ★

It was December 7, 1941, a Sunday afternoon. Pa and I were listening to the radio. I wasn't paying much attention as I played with my Lincoln Logs on the flowered-linoleum floor, building a fort, a US Cavalry outpost. A place to which the Lone Ranger and Tonto raced to report the Apaches were on another warpath. Just like the episode I saw in the serial at the Fox Theater—just before the main feature with Abbot and Costello, who made me laugh so hard I almost peed my pants.

"Listen," Pa says. "Everybody listen! The president's talkin'!"

"FDR?" Ma asks from the kitchen.

"Who else?" Pa answers.

The president talked about the Japanese attacking Pearl Harbor that morning.

"What the hell." Pa says in almost a whisper. "Damned if we ain't at war."

Then, one after another, all the boys in the neighborhood go off to war in France or England or Italy or to islands in the South Pacific nobody ever heard of. Pa got a deferment because the factory he worked in made parts for submarines instead of for Ford cars. He wanted to go fight "Japs" and "Nazis" too, but he was foreman of an assembly line and was labeled "indispensable" for training and supervising the women stepping in for the men.

A year later, I was peddling newspapers on Bill Gottshalk's old route. Billy got killed in France, a place he never thought he'd get to see.

"At least he got to see Paris," his ma said to a neighbor who stopped by when she saw the flag with the gold star in Gottshalk's window.

All along my paper route flags hung in windows, most with blue stars. Here and there, flags with gold stars were hanging. The women who sadly but proudly hung the flags with gold stars are called Gold Star Mothers and rode in the newest cars in town for all the parades. Their boys played football and basketball on the high school teams.

A lot of things changed because of the war. Rubber has been replaced with canvas for your overshoes. The Big Three made planes and warships instead of cars. In the movies, cowboys and Indians shooting each other were replaced by American soldiers shooting Japs and Nazis. And the *Lone Ranger* serial was replaced by *The Eyes and Ears of the World* with mostly pictures of the war and the war effort, narrated by Lowell Thomas, all for ten cents. Food was scarce and gasoline scarcer—both rationed. A huge black market for ration stamps flourished.

I sold defense stamps to the customers on my *Eagle Star* paper route. Ten or twenty-five cents apiece, with a free book to paste them in. When my book had eighteen dollars and seventy-five cents worth of stamps, I traded it in for a war bond for which the government promised to pay twenty-five dollars in ten years.

Every Friday I dismounted my bike, knocked on doors, and collect twenty-five cents for the paper. "Any defense stamps this week, Mrs. Gottshalk?"

All the collecting took place in the doorway or just inside the house; I could always hear the radio playing. Radios played all day in case news of the war came on. I heard so much radio music, I knew all the words to songs like *G.I. Jive, To Each His Own, Lili Marlene, Ole Buttermilk Sky, Elmer's Tune, I'll Be Seeing You and White Cliffs of Dover.* And nobody missed the evening news with Walter Winchell's staccato delivery and a telegraph key clicking in the background. Or Gabriel Heatter with, "Ah, there's bad news tonight," or "good news" if the war is going well.

Customers leafed through the paper to find Ernie Pyle's column reporting news from the front. His two cartoon characters, Willie and Joe, would be crouched in a foxhole, all muddy and wet with rain pouring down on their GI helmets.

"You know, Willie," Joe says. "It does sound like rain on a tin roof."

After the Second World War the economy and educational opportunities boomed. The G.I. Bill gave veterans access to higher education, and they took advantage of that access. My college days were enhanced by those veterans who added their maturity and experiences to my education.

Jobs were plentiful as our country tried to rebuild and supply all those commodities unavailable during the war. Automobiles, refrigerators, rubber products rolled off the assembly lines of factories to salespeople who were in demand to sell them. The middle class prospered.

When I bought a cottage on a lake, my neighbors were carpenters, small-business owners, printers, electricians, clerks in stores and others without a college education or a 401-k. Blue-collar workers, the *middle class*, were buyers of a lifestyle now pretty much in the reach of only the college educated. I would join their ranks, scaling the walls of academia and settling in the sunshine of Florida upon retirement, in relative obscurity, until I picked up my pen, again.

★ ☆ ★

In my family we cousins were called by the diminutives of our names. Donald was called "Donnie", Bob was called "Bobby", Jim was "Jimmy" and I was "Dickie".

My mother and father were well liked and consequently given diminutives also. Russell and Alice were called "Russie" and "Allie".

We cousins played together a lot when we were young. I was the oldest, four years older than Jimmy, who was next in line. He and I were good pals until we became teenagers and drifted apart. Until a few weeks ago Jimmy and I had neither seen nor heard about each other for seventy years. We had no idea of each other's whereabouts. The morning after a conversation with my daughter and son-in-law about family members we had lost track of, my telephone rang.

"Hello."

"Hi, is this Richard J. Smith?"

"Yes."

"Do the names *Russie* and *Allie* mean anything to you?"

"They were my parents."

"You from Marinette?"

"Yeah."

"Hi Dickie. This is Jimmy."

"I'll be dammed!"

Jimmy explained that his wife of many years had died several months previously. One of his daughters gave him a book wherein the author, an old man, had written about the death of his wife and his attempts to recover from his grief. The book was titled *Musings of an Old Man*. Jimmy's daughter thought her dad might find some comfort in reading about another old man grieving for his lost wife. Jimmy didn't know how she came to possess the book.

Jimmy saw the name of the author, Richard J. Smith, but made no connection to me. As he read, he began to wonder if Dickie Smith might have written those pages. When he came upon the name, *Jeannine,* he recalled that cousin Dickie had married a woman by that name. He saw that Richard J. Smith lived at Westminster Retirement Community in Bradenton, Florida, found my number and called.

Let me tell you that his call was a welcome reunion after seventy years. We chatted for an hour, exchanged email addresses, phone numbers and what we each knew about other family members. Jimmy was just one of several who had told me that book was comforting to them. The last was a friend who told me she had read a poem from *Musings* at her husband's memorial service. He and I had been good friends for thirty years. And, somehow, I like to think he heard it.

II.

A TWILIGHT HOUSE

Sometimes sunsets make me sad.
They signal the end of a beautiful day.
Darkness snuffs out sunshine.
Another from my storehouse of days is gone.
What will tomorrow bring?
Might rain replace today's sunshine?
What might the hours of darkness deliver?
Hope is my only prayer for another day of sunshine.
For there is a power far greater than I
Who moves the sun and the moon.
Our clocks do no more than measure
The heartbeats of time.

I now call where I live a *Twilight House.* It is more descriptively called a *Continuing Care Retirement Community* (CCRC). That name has evolved from what was once called—*a nursing home* or *old folk's home.* But CCRCs are more than just a euphuism. They comprise units for *independent living, assisted living* and *skilled nursing* under one roof, or in our CCRC in three buildings.

Jeannine and I moved here six years ago when her dementia required a lifestyle I couldn't provide in a single-family home. We left a house in Wisconsin and a condominium in Florida to finish our lives in a CCRC where our needs were provided by others. Turned out it was a good move, and I soon learned it was a good move for others as well.

When we residents take our meals together in our dining rooms, we often discuss our reasons for moving here. When conversation at the dinner table slows I sometimes ask, "Did you ever think at this time of your life you would be eating here?" Invariably, the answers are "No!" Often the conversation picks up with talk about how and why we're here.

Most stories are similar. An unanticipated diagnosis, a death, the urging of children, the acknowledgement of need for a lifestyle change, simply old-age fatigue. "We were happy where we were until . . ."

Most residents had investigated a variety of retirement communities before settling on ours. Some chose Westminster Bradenton because they have friends or family in the area; few had difficulty choosing among those they investigated. They felt good or they didn't. Ours felt best.

The faith-based and non-profit aspects appealed to many. So did the dining rooms, the quality of the food and the menu choices. Location, activities and the satisfaction of current residents played a role. Some factor or factors determined their choices.

The conversations remind me of a Shakespearian quotation from the play, *Julius Caesar.*

Brutus says to Caesar, "There is a tide in the affairs of men which, taken at the flood, brings fortune." The context in the play is quite different. But at one time in our lives we all rode a tide to Westminster, Bradenton. And we have the good fortune to enjoy our older years together in harmony, friendship, comfort and knowledge that we will be cared for as long as we need care.

I often have to explain why I refer to our CCRC as a *twilight house*, which I often do.

In a poetic sense that's what it is. Those of us here are in our sunset years. The sun still shines on us, but the night is not far away.

We contemplate our lives as holly hocks might,
Grown too tall to see the ground that gave them birth.
We too have lost sight of the ground from which we rose.
Now our growth is over, no longer reaching skyward.
Soon the snow and winds of winter will bend us to the ground,
And we will return to the soil that gave us life.

We know we are old. How? I surveyed my friends and neighbors who admit to being old.

This is a distillation of what they told me:

- I can feel myself growing old, and I could not when I was younger. The difference between eighty-six and eighty-seven is closer, and is traveled faster than the distance between seventy-six and seventy-seven. I close my eyes now and another year has passed. Each year brings greater changes in me and my lifestyle than earlier years did.
- I forget more and need to rely more on my calendar and notes I make myself.

- When I hurt myself or have surgery, I take longer to heal.
- I am more reserved in my behavior, more cautious about what I say and do. I am unsure about my behavior, especially with younger people.
- I am not so driven to be the best at everything I do.
- Living in a small apartment seems sufficient now. The house I moved from was getting too big.
- I rely on more rest periods and naps. I can't work as long or as hard as I once could.
- I can empathize more with people my age. I know what they are going through when they have difficulties of one kind or another. I am not so critical of others anymore.
- I am more insecure about almost everything—my health, my activities, my personal relationships and my driving. I don't trust myself as much as I did when I was younger.

So, there are indeed pluses and minuses to growing old. Those who deny being old miss out on the pluses, but they still suffer the minuses.

When people are searching for the *just-right* twilight house, they often are unaware of what is good about living in one. Of course, the meals, cleanliness and view are important, but it's the folks who live there, and the staff, who make a twilight house good.

Every twilight house has a soul, or a spirit—a feeling of sharing life, camaraderie, belonging. We are diverse in many ways, but we are homogeneous in many more. We have had families, lost friends and loved ones, laughed at life, cried at life, and survived the tempest of youth.

We made it!

We stand together as survivors of a generation quickly becoming history. And in a twilight house we stand together. Loneliness is a burden that can devour the spirit as cancer devours the body. Loneliness afflicts children and young adults, but it is more prevalent in older people.

As time passes, people collect more of what can be lost. All of us here have a long list of losses. The experience of loss binds us together. We have learned to recognize the cancer of loneliness in our neighbors, and their coping with that burden helps us cope with ours. No one is immune.

So, I am thankful that I have chosen to live where loneliness is prevalent, but not in control, where neighbors and staff exemplify and teach that loneliness doesn't have to be in control, that the human spirit is resilient, that loneliness is unavoidable but bearable. We live in a community that gives evidence to the strength of life. We may be down, but we're not out. We have mastered the strength to see the sunshine through the clouds. And we do that better with others than we would do alone.

It is not unusual for people growing uncomfortable in their single-family home to ask me, what it's like at Westminster Point Pleasant, the official name of our twilight house. They are for the most part, people in their eighties and people who have experienced a warning sign of some kind—a fall, a heart attack, a stroke, an accident in the kitchen, an automobile accident or questions from their children regarding their well-being living as they are.

Some of the inquiries are from family and friends, some are from people who have read my books, *Life After Eighty* and/or *Musings of an Old Man*. And, of course, I take questions at appearances I make at gatherings for prospective residents sponsored by our marketing department.

I received a phone call one evening from long-time friends in another state. They are a couple in their mid-eighties. She was having significant problems with her vision, and he was experiencing mobility issues that couldn't be corrected. Their children had encouraged them to sell their home and move to a safer place for the duration of their old age. They investigated and found a CCRC not far from where they lived.

I had encouraged them to investigate several more, just to be sure. Proximity to former neighbors or children is not necessarily the most important variable in choosing a twilight house. And I gave them some other factors to investigate:

1. staff/resident ratio
2. tenure of executive director
3. results of resident satisfaction surveys
4. costs of entry fees and monthly fee
5. transportation
6. social activities
7. quality and quantity of food served
8. pace of serving in the dining rooms
9. dress code
10. housekeeping services
11. security
12. access to nurses and other medical services
13. cleanliness
14. education level of senior administrative staff

And that's enough! You really won't know if you have made a good move for six months or more after the move.

All new residents experience a transition period. That's why it's good to know the refund period for return of all or part of the entry fee. Because of the experience my wife had and I am still enjoying,

I am biased in regard to the best place for most folks to spend their old ages. I think quality twilight houses are the best choice, better than living with children, having children live with you or having caregivers give assistance in family homes.

After eighty, and sometimes before, almost everyone is adversely affected physically and cognitively. Body and mind wear out. Some advertisers, some physicians, some fitness proponents, and even some people over eighty like to think that proper nutrition, lots of exercise and eight hours of sleep a night will keep anyone from growing old. *That's denial!*

Good health habits may give you a better quality of life and, perhaps extend it, but you will still lose cognitive and physical power. We all know someone who is still *with it* at the age of a hundred or more. These are outliers, the anomalies, and they are few. Almost all of us will need or want some assistance to live safely and happily after eighty and certainly before we die.

Some older people resist relocating to a twilight house because they aren't ready. Someone else has to make the decision for them. Some are repelled by the number of residents using canes or walkers—the oldest of our residents. We who see these oldest as neighbors or friends don't notice their dependence on mobility aids. They have become Georges or Sallies, Elaines or Petes. They were attorneys, teachers, nurses, steel workers, store owners, accountants, city workers, salespeople. They are still spouses or widowed persons, parents, grandparents, great grandparents, good people grown old. So, what if they need a walker! Mine will be ready for me when I need it.

When Jeannine died, I was often asked if I would leave the twilight house. I was eighty-six, but active and lucid. *No! Never!* I didn't even entertain the notion of leaving.

My personal clock does not have a backward setting. My past is indeed my past. It is pleasant for me to think about places I have lived and my previous homes. I enjoy talking about cars I have driven, jobs I have held. They are good memories, but I am content to keep them in the past. I am content and happy with what I have, where I am, and who I am, all different from what I had, where I was, and who I was. I will never resettle in a city I once called *home*.

My family and I returned to northern Wisconsin for my deceased wife's burial, where I will be buried when it is my time to join her. We both were born and raised and spent our professional lives there. We lived and worked in various cities and at those times called them *home*. I left each one somewhat reluctantly and thought seriously about returning to one I especially enjoyed for my final years.

One of our grandsons asked me, "Grandpa, how does it feel to be home again?"

He knew how much I enjoyed living in that city and had spoken of someday returning to live there. His question startled me. I was momentarily disoriented.

The city had not changed much since I left, but apparently, I had.

"This isn't home for me anymore," I answered. "When I leave tomorrow, I will be headed home."

I don't know if he understood. Perhaps at the time I didn't. But saying it felt good. I must have meant it. I can return to former homes, but I am not the same and, therefore they wouldn't be either. I don't want to go back.

The twilight house is now my home. I am comfortable, contented, and happy here. I am a canoeist who has no desire to paddle back upstream. Until someone paddles me back to the place I once called home, I will stay here for the remainder of my old age.

III.

NO GOING BACK

Every generation lives through a revolution of some kind. I remember my dad saying he didn't know why people had to fly around in airplanes. His 1935 Ford took him wherever he wanted to go, which was never more than fifty miles to Green Bay and back. On each of those excursions he had either a tire blow out or the fuel pump malfunction. Spare tires and an extra fuel pump were always taken along for those long trips.

Dad didn't understand the world I was growing up in. I could make a telephone call without telling an operator to connect me to someone else's number. I could fly anywhere in the world. I drove cars I didn't have to shift. The music I listened drove him nuts . . . and on and on. Well guess what? I am now where he was then.

Historians divide the evolution of civilization into *Ages*. Examples include *The Stone Age, The Copper Age, and the Iron Age.* Each age is best described by the forces and factors that characterize that particular period of years. So I got to thinking about the forces and factors that seem to describe our age.

Are we perhaps the age of *The Twitter?* Or *The Age of the Ford 150 Truck?* How about *The Age of Fast Food Franchises?* None of those seemed to work for me. So I was still searching when a friend and I went to the beach one evening to listen to music and drink cold beer. And then it came to me!

Have you been downtown on a Saturday afternoon or to the beach lately? If so, you would be overwhelmed by the young bodies covered by tattoos. Not little hearts pierced by an arrow tattoos, or anchors, or the name of a sweetheart and his or her telephone number. Instead, bodies are blanketed in ink with shapes, figures and colors that resemble the descriptions in Milton's *Paradise Lost.* I don't know how they stay hydrated with all the holes punched in them by their tattoo artists. And no one is looking at or talking to each other, either. Their faces are pressed into their cell phones.

It was that scene that lead me to dub current times as *The Tattoo Age* or, alternatively, *The Cell Phone Age.*

We are overpopulated now. I have never added up all the times I have been kept waiting. Probably years if you count the nine months I spent waiting to be born. I am waiting right now in the waiting room of Harold's Auto Repair. I came in an hour ago for my appointment to have an oil change for my car. I never before had to make an appointment or wait at Harold's.

Harold told me when I came in that they were backed up, and that I might have to wait more than an hour. He didn't say how long "more than an hour" might be.

I was leafing through some old magazines, completely uninteresting to me for about twenty minutes when I decided to write this piece. So I have been here over an hour now and have only two short paragraphs to show for it. I hope Harold doesn't run out of clean oil before my car is on the rack. Harold has only one rack.

Harold has finally just come in to the waiting room and was headed my way. *I'll bet my car is ready.*

"Mr. Smith?"

"Yes."

"Bad news."

"Yes?"

"Yep. You need new brake linings. Your battery is shot. I recommend a chassis alignment, and I wouldn't drive far on those tires if I was you."

"And the oil?"

"Should do the other stuff first."

I thought for a quick minute.

"How much and how long?"

"Eight hundred bucks and six hours, maybe a few minutes more. Wanna come back tomorrow?"

"No, I'll wait. I won't have enough money left to go anywhere."

★ ☆ ★

A Walgreens cashier wished me a "Totally awesome rest of the day." It was almost noon and I didn't think I had enough time or energy to accomplish that. So I had a good day. That was good enough for me.

I like the word *good*. It's a good word. Unfortunately, it's going the way of cars that need drivers. Nobody wants to be *good* anymore. Everybody wants to be *great*. Tell somebody he or she did a good job, and he or she is offended. *Good* has come to mean adequate or barely passing. Only *great, fantastic, stupendous or awesome* is a compliment. *Good* is like getting a *C* on your report card. Everybody wants an *A*.

So I have decided to go with the flow. No more, "Have a good day" from me. I want everybody who reads this to have a *GREAT* day. However, I will probably continue saying *goodnight* when I leave someone after dark. *Greatnight* just doesn't sound good.

I don't know if you have noticed, but nobody greets anyone any more without also inquiring as to their wellbeing. "Good morning. How are you today?" Or, "How ya doin'?" I stopped after "Good morning" the other day and the person I greeted said, "Fine, thank you."

I get the feeling that most people who ask how I am don't really give a rip. Doesn't matter because I suspect they don't listen to my reply.

"How ya doin'?"

"Awful, I think I'm going to throw up."

"That's nice. Have a good day."

That's another thing. No well-wisher can will me to have a good day. How could I when I'm on my way to the dentist, or I have to pay a parking ticket at city hall, or my golf game was cancelled because of rain, or I agreed to pick up someone I don't even like at the Tampa airport in a thunderstorm.

"Thanks for the thought, stranger. But how in blazes am I supposed to have a good day?"

★ ☆ ★

Have you noticed that young people talk too fast? I think it's an extension of their texting technique. Their tongues now move as fast as their fingers do. And they don't bother with vowels. They speak as they text—only consonants needed.

New Year's Eve a waitress came to take our orders. She rattled off all the specials, the price of each, and I think, the *Star Spangled*

Banner before I was safely planted on my chair. I ordered a hamburger and fries because I couldn't understand a word she said and I couldn't understand the menu either. I was pretty sure there was a burger and fries in there somewhere.

Whatever happened to adjusting rate, pitch, pause and volume, especially for old folks? There are no variations in the speech of these kids. All their words sound the same to me, just like those of the singers and rappers they listen to. They all need some tongue-adjustment exercises by a speech therapist.

And I would like to know why the least articulate employees end up at reception desks and in customer service departments. They should be assigned to computers—not telephones. Speaking of telephones, I played a garbled message left on my answering machine. All I could make out was, "It is very important that you call" . . . an undecipherable list of numbers followed. I played it again and again, ear pressed to the machine. *Still unclear.* Now I will never know if I missed an important appointment, missed a call from a long-lost friend, or was saved from a phony scheme to steal all my money.

I don't know about you, but the world is going too fast for me, I can't catch my breath!

Maybe it all started with jet travel. Remember how pleasant air travel used to be? Not anymore. It took a long time to receive a letter, but wasn't it more meaningful to receive a letter than an email or Tweet? Long-distance telephoning was reserved for births, marriages or death. Now I get telephone solicitations from India, Indonesia and other places I can't spell several times a day. I prefer hearing from someone who has something to say.

I will end my tirade with modern music and the way some singers render the *Star Spangled Banner* and my favorite Christmas carols.

★ ☆ ★

I like to watch old movies on Channel 53—Taylor Classic Movies. People dressed up in the 20's, 30's and 40's. White collar men wore suits with vests, shirts with ties and always a hat, even on weekdays. Women wore long dresses, covered their heads and wore swimming suits that covered a lot more than swimming suits today cover.

When I began teaching in 1953, we were required to wear shirts and ties and coats in the classroom. Our students dressed up too. Nurses wore white dresses and caps, and physicians always wore white coats. You could tell the people who took care of you from the maintenance workers.

Language that was reserved for *Men Only* places is no-longer reserved. Have you seen an R-rated movie lately, watched a TV sitcom or walked down a busy street? My, my, my, such colorful talk. Even our comic strips have resorted to references to body parts and body function for humor. On sitcoms a flushed toilet is a cue for the laugh track.

Politicians shout at each other, call each other derogatory names and level accusations without evidence that the candidate from the other party is really a dirty rat! Should we be concerned? Perhaps. Margaret Mead, noted anthropologist, warned that societies that lose their *shock value* are in danger of losing their civility. If we examine our media, mass and social, our politics, our language, our dress and other aspects of our society, we must wonder where we are headed. Are we losing respect for ourselves and our fellow citizens? Are we becoming more *uncivilized*, strong as that word may sound?

The likelihood we will stop our tendency toward the elimination of social boundaries, toward the less-restrained morality is slight. But I would like to try what seems to me the easiest beginning. I would like to require business dress for teachers and school uniforms for elementary and secondary school students. I would also require white uniforms and caps for registered nurses and white coats for physicians on duty.

Of course, I would be sued by organizations for teachers, nurses and physicians, and it probably wouldn't work anyway. What did Margaret Mead know?

How in the heck did we manage to get through our childhoods without TV, cell phones and other electronic devices? How boring those years must have been for us. We had to play outdoors—even in the winter. We were forced to build snowmen, slide downhill on sleds, ice skate, have snowball fights and go skiing. Indoors, we listened to the radio, played board and card games, read comics and books we checked out of the library. We even played Tiddlywinks and sang songs we were taught in school and by our grandparents or listened to phonograph records. BORING!

In the summer all we had to do was play kick the can, hopscotch, jacks, baseball, ride our bicycles, go swimming, roller skate, jump rope and play hide and seek until the street lights came on. We read in the summer too. CAN YOU IMAGINE?

Today's kids got it great. They don't need to run around outside, read books, play games with other kids. They don't even have to talk to each other. They can just sit, play games by themselves and type messages to each other long distance. What a life!

I admit I watch too much television. I should read more. And I should eat less and exercise more too. Nobody's perfect. That said, I would like to protest the repetition of TV commercials. I am tired of watching the mayhem guy selling Allstate Insurance by destroying everything in his path. Ditto the little green gecko I used to find cute. Also the man who tells his wife some insurance company doesn't hold grudges like she does.

"What do you have in your wallet" sounded clever the first ten or twenty times I heard it. Now its repetition has worn a hole in my back pocket.

My pillow puts me to sleep without buying one. Now the inventor of that headrest is hawking sheets all day long on every channel. And how many times have I been advised that one Aleve works better than a whole bottle of Tylenol. And "Those who know, know BDO." I am not one who knows.

I do know that like all my other complaints, this one will go unheeded. But at least I am going to get it off my mind . . . Okay, I admit it. I have become a curmudgeon. It took me eighty-nine years, but I'm there! That's the way it is.

I have traded having a *blast* for a nice time on a pleasant afternoon. I watch boring television and feel productive doing it. Some mornings I don't bother shaving. I wear white socks with dress trousers and athletic shoes the color that matches the socks. I tell everybody how much I paid for stuff, when my family is coming to visit, how old I am and that my knees hurt—my feet hurt too. That's why I wear athletic shoes. I even give descriptions of the pills I take and how often I take each one to anyone who will listen. I'm no different from my twilight house neighbors.

No more out to dinner or a movie at night. I go out to lunch and matinees only. There is nothing I want to eat or to see badly enough to get me out after dark. And I don't drive on busy highways or streets anymore—makes me nervous. Besides, there is no place I want to go. As far as I am concerned. I have seen it all and done it all!

I was telling this to a friend who said, "Sounds to me like you've turned into an old—"

Well, I won't repeat exactly what he said, but I like *curmudgeon* or even *geezer* better.

IV.

TWILIGHT POEMS

In my twilight house almost everything is done for me, leaving me with little I need to do. So I write poems. Some of them turn out pretty well, but I always write with a wastebasket next to my chair. I have included some that escaped the round-file, but like beauty, poetry is also in the eye of the beholder. I hope you find a smile or a tear in each of them. They have all been published in one of our two twilight house periodicals.

Let's start with a few smiles.

JUST THINKIN'

My youth is gone, and I want it back.
I'm tired of being old, forgetting things,
Always stiff and sore, afraid of falling.
I want to be young again!
Go to school and pass exams, search for jobs.
I want to start a family, change diapers again.
I want to worry about paying bills, sending kids to college
and . . .
On second thought,
I want to change my mind.

WHO ARE YOU?

I looked in my mirror, and what did I see?
I saw an old man looking back at me.
"Who are you?" I wanted to say.
"Get out of my mirror. Please go away."
But he refused to leave, that grizzled, old guy.
He clung to the glass, until by and by,
I decided he was now who I would see,
Whenever I wanted to take a look at me.
What good is a mirror that tells you a lie?
When you're looking for you, you see some old guy.
So I threw it away, over and done!
Maybe one of these days I'll buy a new one.

FOOD FOR THOUGHT

I know I'd be a whole lot thinner,
If I skipped dessert after dinner.
And salt, I know, is bad for me.
So is coffee and maybe tea.
Add to that wine and beer;
There goes my Christmas cheer.
I'd be a healthy son-of-a-gun,
But I wouldn't be having a whole lot of fun.

Ware's Creek meanders past my window to the Manatee River, to Tampa Bay and the Gulf of Mexico. It carries with it the thoughts, memories, fears, pain and aspirations of twilight house residents.

WARE'S CREEK

I ponder the dark water from my window
And wonder how many others have done as I am doing.
How many on a sleepless night
Have dozed at their windows overlooking Ware's Creek?
How many have turned to those waters with their problems?
How many have confessed their sins to Ware's Creek,
Sat on benches on its banks and relived days long gone?
It may be small, still and little traveled;
But floating boats is not its mission.
It is there for souls like me to find comfort in its permanence.
We may come and go, but Ware's Creek just keeps listening.

NIGHT LIGHTNING ABOVE
WARE'S CREEK

Flashing across the sky
Like a riderless, white stallion.
Through dark, roiling clouds.
Hurling down javelins of light.
Powerful, untamed, thunderous.
A manifestation of the turbulence of nature.
The restlessness of unknown space,
Raising questions of the universe,
The what, how, why of creation.

ONE NIGHT

I awakened one night from a storm of dreams.
One after another they disturbed my sleep.
I was lost. I was falling, threatened by people I didn't
know.
Who are these people? Where are those places?
Why do they haunt me like apparitions from a life I've
never lived?
So now I am awake.
Shall I return to sleep in hope of better dreams?
Or shall I sit by my window and watch daylight chase
the night away
Over Ware's Creek?

Just below my window is a small dock with benches. Small pontoon boats load and unload residents for cruises up and down the Manatee River, one of the amenities with living on Ware's Creek.

Our skilled nursing unit is housed in a wing of the building I live in. It is home to long-term and terminally ill patients as well as patients requiring short-term rehabilitation. My wife spent her last thirty days there, and I have received short-term rehab there for knee replacements. Wheelchairs with patients come and go from that unit all day long. A favorite destination for those in wheelchairs is the dock.

OUT MY WINDOW

One by one they come in pairs,
Old women, old men in wheelchairs,
Pushed by volunteers, friends or family,
Many nearly as old as those they are pushing.
Those in the chairs have outlived their mobility
And now depend on those who have not.
They come to the south dock from the Health Center.
They are there to sit in the sun and watch the pelicans fish.
What are they thinking, those in their chairs?
Do they dream of days long gone, when they were the pushers?
Do they try to imagine the days to come?
Perhaps they will be happy to return to the security of their rooms,
In their chairs, in front of the TV, waiting for their dinners to come.

OF WHAT DO YOU DREAM?

What do you dream of, old man asleep in your chair,
chin on your chest, glasses askew?
Do you dream of your lost love, your fading eyesight,
things gone wrong?
Or are you dreaming of another place, a Shangri-la of dreams.
Where loneliness, pain and worry are unknown?
And I must wonder, as I watch you there, asleep in your chair,
Will you be relieved when you awaken? Or would you prefer to
stay with your dreams?

Our Florida sunsets are spectacular. Tourists from all over the world travel here to sit on our beaches and watch.

ANOTHER SUNSET

Sunsets make me melancholy.
A day is gone that will never return.
I have spent another twenty-four hours.
The passage of time is the drumbeat of life.
Sunrise, Sunset. Fiddler on the Roof.
Yesterday, today, tomorrow.
Days, week, decades
Slide away from my allotted years.
And each sunset I am reminded
That my time is growing shorter.

We old-timers look at our children now and see them differently from how we saw them when they were young. And we now know that the circle of life will bring them around to where we are now. We are born, we grow old and we die. One generation steps aside and another takes its place.

THOUGHTS AT A GRANDSON'S WEDDING

Tonight I weep for my lost youth,
My limber movements, sure of foot.
Moving with a confidence now gone.
I dreamed a future, long and productive.
Now my future is short and uncertain.
I watch those I once was as they dance by.
And I remember when I danced as they do now.
We have traded places, they and I.
And someday they will do as I do now,
Sit, watch, admire, remember.
And they will weep for their lost youth.

Sometimes it is difficult to see our children all grown. We try to remember.

DEAR CHILDREN

We look at you with your children and grandchildren
And try to remember:
The day we brought you home from the hospital,
How we fed you, rocked you, diapered you.
How we taught you to walk,
Celebrated your birthdays and Christmases,
How we bought you bicycles, took you to school,
Watched you graduate and find jobs.
Now you see us, growing old and dependent,
In need of the care we once gave you.
Babies and old folks are the story of life.
Everything God made has a beginning and an end.
Once we were babies too.

Sometimes trying to remember brings regrets.

A PRAYER FOR THOSE FOR WHOM THE SUN HAS SET

Some would do it all the same;
Others would not.
For those who would not,
I offer this prayer:
I hope where you are,
All is better now.
Hopefully you have been able to
Make amends,
Say what you should have said,
Apologize for what you should not have.
I hope you are holding hands
With those you disliked.
Forgiven those you should have forgiven.
This life is filled with imperfection.
I must believe the next is not.
All enmity gone.
All sorrow relieved.
Illnesses healed.
Weaknesses strengthened.
Misunderstandings now understood.
That is my prayer.
For are there not things we all should have done,
But did not?
And some things we should not have done,
But did?

And I try to remember the little things.

> *If I had my life to live over,*
> *I would pay more attention to the little things.*
> *Now I am visited by memories filled with holes,*
> *Wisps of days gone by.*
> *I have forgotten:*
> *The crying of my babies,*
> *The sound of her voice,*
> *The smells of her kitchen,*
> *Holding my children on my lap,*
> *Reading them stories . . .*
> *Now all dim remembrances.*
> *What seemed unimportant then*
> *Seems important now.*
> *Was I there?*
> *Of course I was there.*
> *But I wasn't paying attention,*
> *To the little things.*

And sometimes I am visited by a pleasant memory.

> *I dreamed last night*
> *That I was young again.*
> *How old?*
> *I don't know,*
> *Maybe thirteen or fourteen.*
> *I could run again, play ball, ride my bike.*
> *My first girlfriend, Greta,*
> *Sat with me on her front porch swing.*
> *And at the age of eighty-nine,*
> *I felt again my first lover's kiss.*

I recall a poignant moment.

> *I'm lonely tonight.*
> *Shall I give you a call?*
> *I'm sorry we quarreled*
> *Over nothing at all.*
> *Maybe you're lonely,*
> *As lonely as I.*
> *Let's get together,*
> *Let bygones go by.*
> *I'm holding my phone.*
> *I have no other choice.*
> *For I really must hear*
> *The sound of your voice.*

And I think of you.

> *There's a longing that won't go away.*
> *Down deep, silent and dark.*
> *The voice, gait, smile, laugh.*
> *All gone.*
> *A new life, a different me.*
> *Yet sometimes a song, a sunset, a rainy day,*
> *And the past returns, like a mist.*
> *A picture, not sharp, not clear,*
> *A faint image of what once was.*
> *There's a longing that won't go away,*
> *Down deep, silent and dark.*
> *And it comes and goes, like the night.*

And then we try to forgive ourselves . . .

I have decided never again to regret something I have done in the past. *Why did I? Why didn't I? I should have. I should not have. I will never again . . .* The last one makes sense. I can act differently in the future—I can learn from the past experiences I now regret.

"What's done is done and cannot be undone." A quote from Macbeth. Why stew about something I cannot change? Let it rest. Just don't do it again. Regrets are all about something done at an earlier time in our lives. We weren't the same persons we are now. Now we are more experienced, wiser, not as busy with other matters—different people. The circumstances that played into whatever we did or didn't do will never be the same. Forgiving ourselves and moving on is a better choice than gnawing on bones of regret. *P.S.* It doesn't always work.

I started this chapter with a few smiles, and I would like to conclude the chapter with another smile. I was a teacher for forty years.

APRIL FOOL!

First day in April, clear 'cross the nation,
All children in school declared a vacation.
Instead of doing their spelling and stuff,
They stood up and shouted, "We've worked quite enough!"
"For years now we've toiled with paper and pen.
We now declare never to do that again.
We're now going to start a new kind of school,
Where fun and games and tricks are the rule."

Their teachers were speechless, shocked to the core.
They never had seen this behavior before.
They watched as kids wrestled and played catch with books,
Completely ignoring their teachers' stern looks.

"Stop this right now," their teachers all pleaded,
But not even one of the school children heeded
The pleas of their teachers. They fell on deaf ears,
And were answered only with rudeness and jeers.

"Well," said the teachers, "there's nothing to do,
But join in these games and have some fun, too."
So much to the children's surprise and chagrin,
All over the country teachers joined in.

They threw paper airplanes clear cross the room,
And drummed on wastebaskets—Perdinkel, Perboom!
Pieces of chalk they rolled down the aisles.
Drew faces with frowns instead of with smiles.

They spun the globe 'till it made the kids dizzy.
When the children cried, "Teach!" they said, "We're too busy,
We're having ourselves a ball, can't you see?
Come on! Let's all dance, Ta-Ra-Whoop-Dee-Dee."

They pounded erasers under kids' noses,
And sat on their desks in funny, clown poses;
Scribbled on maps, on blackboards, on pages;
Even let gerbils out of their cages.

The children then said, "Please stop all these tricks.
We really wish you would not try to mix
Being teachers with mischievous fun.
The two together just cannot be done."

"What, what?" said the teachers, "what's all this fuss?
We like your new school. It's super for us.
Not to plan lessons, correct all those papers.
We're ready and willing to keep up these capers."

The children were worried and looked kind of sick.
Not one of them wanted to play one more trick.
"We wish," said the children, "that you'd kindly lead
Us back to our old ways." The teachers agreed.

The school children learned a lesson that day;
Sometimes work can be more fun than play.
They also learned that it's really no kick
To be on the other end of a trick.

V.

COMFORT

You had a dream, dear
I had one too.
Mine was the best dream
Because I dreamed of you.

Remember that old song? Can you still sing or hum it? So how do you feel about dreams? Some people tell me they never dream. I don't know if I envy them or not. Some nights I have really bad dreams, and some nights they're pretty good. Most of them are a hodgepodge of nonsense. When I awaken from a good one, I try to go back to sleep in case it might still be there. When I awaken from a bad one, I am glad I am no longer where I was seconds ago.

Often, I have a dream and know I had one, but can't remember it. The more I try to get it back, the farther away it moves. The good ones disappear fast. Sometimes a bad one will hang around until noon or later—like a dark cloud over my head. I don't even remember what the dream was about, but I feel sad anyway.

Many of my dreams are recurring. I can fly just by moving my arms; I need to run, and I can't move my feet. I am falling in an elevator; a beautiful woman is flirting with me—I like that one, but it doesn't come around very often.

> *Come, sweetheart, tell me,*
> *Now is the time.*
> *You tell me your dream,*
> *And I'll tell you mine.*

I'm not sure if I like having dreams or not, but I sure like that song.

I have always envied people who go to bed at 10:00 pm, are sound asleep at 10:02 pm and don't wake up until 6:02 am. How refreshing that must be—eight uninterrupted hours every night.

I was thinking about that at 12:47am one morning when I was unable to fall asleep. I have never been a good sleeper, and getting old hasn't helped. So I was trying to get to sleep by thinking about sleep. It wasn't working. I remembered that arithmetic always made me sleepy in grade school, so I decided to give it a try.

Let's see, if you sleep eight hours a night for a week, you spend fifty-six hours a week *sleeping. And for a month that adds up to 224 hours. Twelve x 224=2,688 hours a year, except leap years. Now, if you live to be ninety . . . Holy Rip Van Winkle!*

I fell asleep, feeling sorry for those poor folks who sleep their lives away.

My advice to those of us lacking slumber is to beware of the two o'clock in the morning worry time. Little problems take on gigantic proportions in the darkness. During various early-morning hours

I have worried about dental appointments, whether I tipped the waitress enough, how I am going to maneuver the traffic on Cortez Road, whether I offended someone in a spirited conversation . . . and on and on.

Forget it! There is nothing anyone can do about anything at two o'clock in the morning.

The dentist's office won't be open for six hours. But you can't forget it! Your mind is stuck, your blood pressure rises, your pulse quickens. DAMN! Why can't I sleep?

Eventually, the sun rises and you find your worries were groundless. What was worrisome now can be easily resolved. *Every cloud must have a silver lining. Wait until the sun shines through.*

So, when you are fretting about something that is really nothing at all at two o'clock in the morning, know that most others are doing the same thing. But just in case I am not awake and fretting that morning, don't call me to see if I am.

Remember this song? *"Love and marriage, love and marriage, go together like a horse and carriage."* That once was true of music and romance—no more I fear.

I can't tell much about the songs young people sing today because of the rate, pitch, and volume of their singing. You can add articulation to that list. But I strongly suspect their love songs are not as lovely as those our generation sang to foster romance.

Remember those love songs we all danced to, cheek to cheek? Here are a few. Hum along with me.

"I know a little bit about a lot of things, but I don't know enough about you." Now those are lyrics that could start an engine.

"I'd like to get you on a slow boat to China." Remember that one?

Eddie Fisher singing *"If I ever needed you, I need you now."* Are you still humming?

Rosemary Clooney: *"Come on-a my house, my house, I'm gonna give you candy."*

"My heart cries for you, sighs for you." Can you still hum that one?

"Because of you there's a song in my heart." Tony Bennett.

"And when we get behind closed door . . ." After marriage, of course.

My all-time favorite, *"I want some red roses [sing it with me] for a blue lady. Mister florist take my order please. We had a silly quarrel the other day. Hope these pretty flowers chase the blues away."* What memories!

I think if our grandkids danced to more of that kind of music, their lives would be—what's the word I'm looking for? Mellow. That's it. Their lives would be more mellow. Maybe colleges should require a course in Music and Romance 101.

How many of you reading this have an easy chair, probably a well-worn recliner you wouldn't part with for any price? Raise your hands. I thought so, almost all of you. Very few old folks don't have one. I have one, and oh how I missed it when I was in our health center for knee-replacement rehabilitation. The chair in my room there was a poor substitute. When I got home, I limped to my chair. "Ah, it's good to be home."

My chair is leather with a handle on the side that elevates a footrest. Makes me smile just thinking about it. I watch TV in it, write and read in it, eat in it, have a beer in it and sleep at least an hour in it every night before I go to bed. It makes my apartment a home.

I have visitors now and then, and I have noticed no visitor ever takes that chair. It doesn't have a *NO VISITORS* sign on it, but everyone seems to know it's off limits. It's my chair, and everybody instinctively sits somewhere else.

My chair is at least thirty years old, and it shows. It's full of indentations that fit only my body parts, and it probably smells like me, which is probably why no one else sits in it. It's an inanimate me.

If you have such a chair, you know what I mean. If you don't, go buy one right away. It takes years before it sinks in just the way you like it and smells like you. And if you spill a little something on it now and then, leave it there. Those spots add character.

Summer is more than a season, more than a number of months, weeks or days on a calendar. Summer is a feeling way down inside of you, a feeling of freedom and play.

"I think I'll knock off work early today. It's summer."

"Look it's nine o'clock and the sun is still out." School is out, time for a vacation. *"Where shall we go this year?"*

"Let me sleep, Ma, it's summer—no school bus."

I don't know why; I just feel better in the summer. *"Batter up!"* Another homerun for the Rays. Who needs a coat? No more snow to shovel. The tourists are gone—let's go to the beach. It's the Fourth of July. Time for a picnic—watch the fireworks—KA BOOM!! WHIZZ—the Stars and Stripes forever! God Bless America.

"Roll out those lazy, hazy, crazy days of summer. Those days of soda and pretzels and beer." Nat King Cole.

"Let's have a picnic."

"Where's the mustard?"

"Hand me a beer."

"Who made this potato salad?"

No, summer is not just a time of year, another season. Some of our happiest memories are of those lazy, hazy, crazy days of summer. Those days of freedom, friendship, picnics, barbecues, hot dogs and beer.

"Let's go swimming."

You can sleep late or get the garden planted.

You can hear the grass grow.

"School's out! School's out!" The days are long; the nights short. Lots of daytime for lots of play time. Time to feel like you never feel other times of the year. It's SUMMERTIME!

Junk closet. You probably have one too. It's filled with things you will never use again, but can't bear to give or throw away.

Mine is filled with empty boxes I might want to put something in someday, flower pots I might want to plant something in someday, old clothes I might want to wear someday, ribbons I might want to put on a gift someday, pieces of rope I might want to tie something with someday, old socks I might find someone to mend for me someday and useless memorabilia that belong in the trash.

We all know none of what we "might do someday" will ever be done. But we just can't throw away stuff with potential usefulness, stuff that gives us comfort.

"Let the kids do it when we are gone." I did it for my parents. You probably did it for yours. I can hear them now saying, *"We'll never use this, but Dick might want it. Put it in the closet with all the other things he, or someone in the family, might find use for—when we're gone."*

I have noticed most of the folks who move in here bring stuff that would be impossible to use in a small apartment. Somehow, having a tea party with service for ten or tableware for a dinner for eight seems unlikely to be used in their three rooms. But we have the equipment—just in case.

I have an L. L. Bean jacket suitable for twenty-below zero weather I brought from Wisconsin—in case we have a cold snap someday. I love that jacket.

"Son, Tony, might want it—when I'm gone." Tony lives in Florida now too. So maybe one of his kids. That jacket is thirty years old, but it hasn't been worn much. It doesn't get down to twenty-below zero in Wisconsin very often, either.

The good news is that psychologists tell us that having things we love near us, even if we never use them, lowers blood pressure. Besides, the kids might find use for them—after we're gone.

VI.

DISCOMFORT

I 'll bet we all have a piece of clothing in our closet or drawer that we are unsure about, a garment that may or not look good on us. I had a shirt like that. Somehow, it didn't seem to be *me*. Then again, I thought I might look great in it. I just didn't know. I'll bet I put that shirt on more than a dozen times, checked it out in a mirror, took it off again and put on another shirt that seemed to be more me.

Soon thereafter, I was going out to dinner with friends, a casual dinner. I felt like wearing something different, so I put that shirt on again, determined to wear it this time—and I did, but I was uncomfortable. It fit okay, but I felt like I was wearing some other guy's shirt. I came up with a whole lot of reasons why I should change it, even as I started my car to drive away. The feeling that I looked like a dope grew stronger as I made my way to the table my friends had reserved. I was sure everyone in the place was staring at me, and I knew my face was flushed.

What the heck, I thought. *They're all friends—and what do I care about the other people in the restaurant? I'll never see them again.*

"Hi, guys." I greeted the group. "How's everyone tonight?" I was sure they all looked stunned by my attire.

"Hi, Dick," several responded. "We're doing great!"

I felt better.

Then one of the women in the group said, "What an interesting shirt."

I felt my face redden and slid into an empty chair. I don't remember anything else about that evening. I could hardly wait to get home and take that damnable shirt off. Maybe by *interesting* she meant it looked great on me. Then again, maybe I looked like I felt in it. I guess I'll never know because I gave that shirt to a friend of mine who volunteers at a shelter for the homeless. So, if you see some homeless man wearing an *interesting* shirt, it was mine. What the heck did she mean by "interesting"?

Some people are procrastinators. They are fearful of making a mistake, I suppose. I was a procrastinator when I was young. Took me forever to decide. That was okay when I was younger. But now I don't have time for that. I move fast about getting things that need doing done.

For example, I had called someone long overdue for a return call from me. I got it done! I paid a bill that wasn't even due. It has become especially important to meet all of my financial obligations. "The road to hell is paved with good intentions." Remember that? Well, I am no longer on that road.

None of us knows how much time he or she has left to procrastinate. "Here today, gone tomorrow." Remember that one? Now's the time to get it done! Today not tomorrow!

So if anyone out there owes me money—PAY UP!

I was having the best conversation the other day when I realized I was talking to myself. I wonder if all single people do that. Maybe even people who live with someone else do that. I don't know. I didn't even know I did it until recently.

Now I catch myself all the time commenting to myself about this and that.

"Wow! Sure is hot out today."

"Sure is. I should have taken the tram."

Then I thanked a dark cloud that came by.

I even talk to inanimate objects. One morning I hurled a profanity at my bed because it had to be made every day. Dirty dishes are always under attack. I say some very nice things to my leisure chair, punctuated by sighs when I sit down and grunts when I struggle to get up.

One evening I caught myself calling to my TV remote, "Where in hell are you?"

I suspect I am not alone in these one-sided conversations. I heard one resident shouting at a balky computer in the computer room the other day. And I heard one resident all by herself reading a newspaper in the library say, "Well, for heaven's sake."

I have heard a lot of solitary muttering at the mailboxes after supper every night. Seems I'm not the only one who gets notices to extend the warranty on a car I sold five years ago.

Well, I have concluded that it's not so bad to talk to oneself . . . if you don't pay too much attention to what is said.

★ ☆ ★

Sometimes I watch the news and am happy my age will protect me from the devastation of the fire and fury prognosticators say will happen if our country continues the course it is on. I don't want to be around if that happens. I want the country to outlive me.

I often change channels and hear different predictions. Politicians and pundits on that channel tell me we are entering a period of enlightenment and prosperity. "Everything's coming up roses . . . " as that old song goes. Then I wish I were younger. I sure hate to miss out on all that great stuff coming down the road.

So not knowing which channel was *fake news* and which was not, I called a history professor friend of mine.

"Which is it?" I asked.

He thought for a minute and answered, "Damned if I know."

This from a man who had proclaimed to know everything as long as I have known him.

"Never was a time in history so unpredictable as the one we are living in. I'm as confused as you are," he confessed.

I figured if he didn't know, nobody knew. So, I decided to spend most of my television time watching a channel that makes me feel optimistic and wishing to be young again. If the dire predictions of the other news channels win out, I won't be around to see it.

Did you ever get a song stuck in your head and not be able to unstick it? Happens to me all the time. I know a lot of songs, well, parts of them.

Usually I know the melodies all the way through, but not all the words. I start a lot of songs I can't finish. So, I sing as far as I can and hum the rest. Sometimes I sing as much as I can and make up words that rhyme, but aren't those Bing Crosby sang. A lot of people get annoyed by that.

"If you can't finish it, don't start it!"

I have no idea why, but the other day *Melancholy Baby* got stuck in my head. Couldn't get it out. I had the words this far:

> *Come to me my melancholy baby,*
> *Cuddle up and don't be blue.*
> *All your fears are foolish fancies, baby.*
> *La-dee, la-dee, la-dee, la-dee, doo.*

I tried repeatedly but couldn't remember that last line. I was still trying at my table, waiting for my BLT with mayo to arrive, when I decided to try singing it, softly so no one would notice. Maybe the words to that last line would somehow pop out. They didn't. So after my *La-dee, da-dee, daas* I stopped. Then I heard a lady's voice from a nearby table.

"*Don't you know that I'm in love with you?*" I kept waiting for her to say, "Now shut up!" But she didn't, bless her heart. I guess that would have been hard for her, having sung those sweet words to me.

It was many decades ago, but I can still hear Sister Mary Rose preparing us for our first confessions before our first communions. The first step was the examination of conscience.

There wasn't a whole lot to find in my third-grade conscience, so I made a few things up, like sassing my mother—sister's suggestion. As I grew older, the task became easier.

> *But when to mischief mortals bend their will,*
> *How soon they find fit instruments of ill.*

—Alexander Pope [1688-1744]

As I grew into adolescence Father and I had more to talk about in the Saturday confessional. That's probably why I refrained from doing the really bad stuff.

Now that was a long time ago, but this old tree is still inclined to examine my conscience now and then and repent.

To err is human, to forgive divine.

—Alexander Pope [1688-1744]

And I am finding, as I near my ninetieth birthday, that my conscience is looking more and more like it did when I was a third grader.

Sometimes my soup will be served cooler than I like. And sometimes I will not receive a Thank You note for a gift I gave. Someone I like will take longer than I like to return an email or pay-off a Super Bowl bet. That's just the way it works. Do I want to shorten my list of people I like? How long will I fret about minor things and subject other people to my fretting? Alas, it is an imperfect world. Voicing my hurt feelings will not change that.

So the next time someone who was seated after you gets served before you, or you are behind some cheat in the express checkout line with more than ten items in his cart, take a deep breath and remind yourself that alas, it's an imperfect world. You will feel better, I promise.

I used to be a complainer. Not a constant or a loud complainer, but I got upset about what were no more than minor inconveniences or injustices. I voiced my displeasure to anyone who would listen.

After years of chastising people for their mistakes or injustices, I realized I was making myself more miserable than those I was chastising. And much of what is done cannot be undone anyway. I concluded that try as I might, I was not going to eliminate human error. I said to myself, "Alas, it's an imperfect world." I immediately felt better. It was no longer my job to perfect the imperfect. Whew! Incompetence and injustice are parts of the human condition.

VII.

MINCING WORDS

A grammarian once told Winston Churchill that he should never end a sentence with a preposition, to which he replied, "This is errant pedantry up with which I shall not put."

That was a long time ago. Now a preposition is just fine to end a sentence with. When a rule of English usage begins to get in the way of effective communication—when it no longer sounds right—it is time to change that rule.

Informal English is now quite acceptable in polite company, and it sounds better. Not many of us say, "It was I." "It was me" sounds better. The formal calls too much attention to itself, even though it is preferred in English grammar books. So does, "Everybody has their tickets." Sounds better than, "Everybody has his or her ticket."

"They all have their tickets" solves the problem. And "None is going" is now heard less frequently than "None are going." Even though *none* is a contraction for *no one*.

Ain't is still a no-no, and so are double negatives. But you can split all the infinitives you want to now. The point is that languages live, and what lives changes. Poets no longer write like William Shakespeare. What was once unacceptable in the rule book becomes acceptable when people who are successful communicators and recognized as such begin to use them. So, feel free to say, "It was me." But not "I don't want none." At least not yet.

★ ☆ ★

I have long been on a mission to simplify communication for speakers of English. I have advocated liberating *ain't* and going easy on the word *love*. Now I want to put *whom* behind locked doors.

"Who are you going with?" comes off the tongue easier than "With whom are you going?"

Whom and whomever are slipping into the category of archaic. Even professional authors and speakers are no longer distinguishing between the nominative and subjective cases. Let's ditch them, except for very formal writing and speech.

My high school students in senior English couldn't keep *who* and *whom* straight, and *whom* was still being used incorrectly in doctoral dissertation I supervised. Making the distinction between *who* and *whom* is simply too difficult to bother with. And really, doesn't "Who are you going with?" sound better than, "With whom are you going?"

Ah! Ha! I suspect some of you (if anyone is still reading) are saying, "Not I. I always use *who* and *whom* correctly." Well, let's see.

In which of the following sentences is the correct case for the pronoun used correctly?

a. I will give the prize to whoever chooses the correct pronoun.
b. I will give the prize to whomever chooses the correct pronoun. (The answer is given at the end of this essay.) Don't look now!

My point is, who cares? Both communicate clearly. Let's do us all a favor and let the nominative case (whoever) work for both. Why go through the work of choosing. The message is the same with either pronoun. Do not be infirm of purpose. Stand with me on this. Let's let *whom* go the way of leisure suits for men and silk stockings with garters for women. We should no longer have to worry about that choice. Okay. Now you can see the answer to that test.

Whoever is the correct choice. It is the subject (therefore nominative case) for the clause that follows the preposition *to*. The entire clause is the object of the preposition *to*. As I said earlier, who cares?

Scottish poet, Robert Burns [1759-1796], wrote in the dialect of his region. He wrote of the common folk and for the common folk and often read his poems in taverns where his readings were always well-received. Folklore had it that Bobby Burns paid for his drinks with his poetry.

One of his best-known poems is *To A Mouse,* and one of the stanzas remains well-known and often quoted today.

> *The best laid schemes o' mice an' men*
> *Gang aft agley*
> *An' lea'e us naught but grief an' pain*
> *For promised joy.*

Less known is the story behind those lines, why Burns compared the trials and tribulations of a mouse to those of men. Prior to that stanza Burns tells of a Scottish plowman who overturns the nest of a mouse, built by the mouse with "Many a weary nibble." The mouse intended the nest to be its home for the winter months.

> *Thou saw the fields laid bare an' waste,*
> *An' weary winter comin' fast,*
> *An' cozie here, beneath the blast,*
> *Thou thought to dwell,*
> *Till, crash! The cruel plow passed*
> *Out through thy cell.*

Burns concludes his poem by comforting the mouse who knows and feels only the present. Men, on the other hand, carry memories of past misfortunes and contemplate future topsy-turvy times in their lives when their best laid schemes will "gang aft agley an' lea'e them naught but grief an' pain for promised joy."

In *To A Louse,* Burns uses his observations of a louse to illustrate that we might behave differently if we could see ourselves as others see us. "O wad some power the giftie gie us to see ourselves as ithers see us."

The louse he uses as illustration is crawling on the tresses of a young woman in church displaying her fine hairdo for those in the pews behind her to envy. She is unaware that they are watching the progress of a louse, more commonly found on poor folk with poor hygiene, making his way in and out of her curls. Burns addresses the louse:

> *I wad na been surprised to spy*
> *You on an auld wife's flannel cap*

Or on some bit ragged boy,
But miss's fine Lunardi! Fye!
How dare ye do't?

Then he cautions the young woman:

O Jenny, dinna toss your head
An' set your beasties all abread!
Ye little know what cursed speed
The beastie's makin!
An' all a us are notice takin!
O wad some power the gifie gie us
To see oursels as ithers see us!
It wad from monie a blunder free us,
What airs in dress and gait wad lea'e us
An ev'n devotion!

The narratives in Burns' poetry move from specific examples in the behavior of all of us to broader generalizations that are relative to the human condition. Do we not all have some of our best laid plans *gang aft aglae*? And might we all not profit from seeing *oursels as ithers see us*?

In a written composition course I taught many years ago a student submitted the following short essay. Every sentence needed a correction. Can you spot the needed corrections?

"My twin sons will graduate high school this June. Bill
is the best student of the two and will graduate with honors.
Neither of them were planning to go to college. However, a

favorite teacher persuaded them quickly to change their minds. The teacher that changed their minds found a scholarship for both of them. Now I am looking forward to watching happily as they graduate college. I will always be thankful to the teacher that found a scholarship for them."

Here is the rewrite:

"My twin sons will graduate from high school this June. Bill is the better student of the two and will graduate with honors. Neither of them was planning to go to college. However, a favorite teacher persuaded them quickly to change their minds. The teacher who changed their minds found a scholarship for both. Now I am looking forward to watching happily as they graduate from college. I will always be thankful to the teacher who found scholarships for them."

1. High schools and colleges don't need to be *graduated*. We *graduate* from them.
2. Twins are two. The comparative—not superlative—adjective is needed.
3. *Neither* is singular. It means *neither one*, therefore, *was*.
4. Teachers are people, so the antecedent *who* not *that*.
5. Graduating *from* a school.
6. Again, persons call for the antecedent *who* not *that*.

Anyone still reading?

I have always found truth in the poetry of Alexander Pope [1688-1744]. For example,

Words are like leaves, and where they most abound,
Much fruit of sense beneath is rarely found.

or

For fools rush in where angels fear to tread.

or

Tis education forms the common mind;
Just as the twig is bent, the tree's inclined.

The first is especially applicable to politicians.

February, the month of Saint Valentine, love and lovers. Remember when we exchanged valentines with all of our classmates in elementary school? We were more selective when we got to high school. After high school I went to college and grew up to be a teacher of literature. In that literature I found love poems you will never find on a Hallmark valentine.

One of my favorites is a Shakespearean sonnet:

"When in disgrace with fortune and men's eyes, I all alone beweep my outcast state . . . Then happily I think of thee, and I would not change my state with kings."

Now what lover would not love to hear that whispered in her or his ear on February 14?

And Robert Browning, of course. "How do I love thee? Let me count the ways." What a disappointment when your loved one's count comes up shorter than yours.

Bobbie Burns, that silver-penned Scotsman, what a lover.

O', my love is like a red-red rose that's newly sprung in June.
O' my love is like a melody that's sweetly played in tune.

SIGH!

I don't know if love poems are being written today by anyone other than greeting-card writers. Does anyone sit down and write a sugary poem to his or her sweetie? Maybe modern music is filled with sweetness. I don't know because I can't understand the lyrics. But I'll bet they can't match Nat King Cole's, *"They try to tell us we're too young. Too young to really be in love."*

I started this piece with a Shakespearean sonnet. I will end it with a scene from Romeo and Juliet.

Juliet emerges from her bedroom just before dawn. She steps to the front of her balcony and sees Romeo standing below, his hand over his heart. She smiles down at him. He looks up at her and says, "Lo, tis the East, and Juliet is the sun." Let's see Hallmark top that one.

VIII.

CHRISTMAS SPIRITS

You may or may not believe in the Christmas Spirit. Some people don't believe in anything they can't see. To them, seeing is believing. But who has seen an angel? Yet would any of us deny the existence of angels? Of course not.

Now I didn't really see the *Christmas Spirit*, but I saw that spirit at work. Yes, I did. It was one Christmas day at my grandparent's house. The whole family was there, and they all saw it too.

I was only a kid, maybe eight or nine. I know I didn't believe in Santa Clause anymore. So, it's not as if I believed in everything you can't see. We were all having Christmas dinner with Grandma and Grandpa. Grandma had cooked a big turkey with all the trimmings, and there were wine and eggnog for the grownups. Maybe that's why the Spirit of Christmas showed up. Anyway, we were all there even though grandpa didn't want to celebrate Christmas that year. He didn't even want a Christmas tree, but Uncle Pete and Aunt Sally got one and put it up because Grandma said Christmas just wouldn't be Christmas without a tree in their living room.

So, Grandpa was the only one who didn't want to celebrate Christmas. He was all recovered from a heart attack, but he wouldn't take the doctor's word that he should get about his life again. I guess he wanted to stay sick. He had been a Marine, *Semper Fi,* and all that stuff. I don't know how many times I saw his medals and was told to join up when I got old enough. Anyway, he was being a jerk about having had a heart attack. I guess he thought Marines shouldn't get sick, figuring he had let the Corps down by having a heart attack. Maybe he thought if he shaved, took his pajamas and robe off, stood up straight and walked without a cane he would have another heart attack. I don't know. Grandma said he was depressed and damned hard to live with.

At Christmas dinner, we all ate ourselves full and went into the living room to open presents, the best part for me. Grandpa said he didn't want any presents that year, but we all got him one anyway. Now here comes the good part:

Uncle Chuck said, "Pa, before we open presents why don't you tell us about the Christmas you spent overseas in Korea." We all had the story memorized, and wanted to get at the presents, but Uncle Chuck asked anyway.

"You damn right I will," Grandpa spouted. "You all get to opening presents. I don't want any anyway. I'll be right back."

Now here's where the Spirit of Christmas comes in.

Grandpa did come back when we were on about the second present. He was all slicked up in his old uniform, medals and all, walking without a cane. He took Grandma by the hand, walked her over to the Christmas tree and said, "Now this here woman is the only present I want. Take a picture of a Marine and his lady at Christmastime. I'm damned glad I ain't in Korea."

I never saw Grandma smiling so hard as when Aunt Sally took her picture. Uncle Pete let out a big, "HOO RAH!" and we all joined in. Uncle Pete had been a Marine too. Now how else would you explain a happening like that if it weren't for the Christmas Spirit.

During World War II, the times were dark and cloudy, but Christmas, like the eastern sky, always brought light. It would be downright unpatriotic not to celebrate Christmas, because celebrating Christmas was one of the things we were fighting to preserve.

The stores were a little short of toys to buy, but Santa's workshop and elves always came through.

A girl (or boy)
Searching for that special toy.
The tree is trimmed.
Its lights are bright.
Can't you see that Christmas sight?"
It's long ago
When you were young.
Your grown-up song is yet unsung.
Hear the bells?
It's Christmas day.
You've asked for toys, so you can play.
Santa's come!
Don't you see
All the presents 'round your tree?

Of course, you saw them. Each gift-wrapped in tissue paper—white mostly, but some green and some red. And tied with colored string. A name tag on each so you wouldn't unwrap a doll instead of a Roy Rogers gun and holster set. Or a dump truck instead of a mirror, brush, and comb set. Not even war stopped Christmas from coming or Pa from buying Ma another bottle of Evening in Paris perfume. Strings popped, tissue paper floated to the floor and settled in multicolored drifts. And you'd forget about the war.

Time for breakfast. Always something special for Christmas morning. Waffles maybe, with no limit on the maple syrup. Eggs and ham if you know a farmer nearby. Chances were Mother has a fresh-baked fruitcake or kuchen. And, of course, decorated sugar cookies shaped like stars, bells and wreaths. A lot of sugar and butter ration stamps had to be spent for those.

Off to church, without Pa 'cause he went to midnight services. Every year you heard the same story. You know it by heart. A baby born in a stable. But not just any baby. This one was God himself. No heat in the stable, so the animals kept Him warm. Angles in the sky—*Hark the Herald Angels Sing* . . . A huge star in the sky spotted by three kings who traced it to the stable.

Round yon virgin, mother and child . . . It was years before I knew what "virgin birth" meant. It was Christmas, and Christmas required faith—faith in the preacher, faith in Santa Claus, faith in the rightness of war. *Oh Come All Ye Faithful* . . .

Church gets long
Try not to sleep.
Eyelids heavy.
Sinking deep.
Pinch yourself.
Give a shake.
You felt that pinch
Now stay awake!

"Let us pray," your pastor would say, "for our men and women in uniform, in Germany, France, Italy, Iwo Jima. On land or sea or in the air. Fighting, offering their lives so we may live free. As Jesus died to save us from eternal damnation." We bow heads and ask God to stop the war—please. Because it is Christmas, and Jesus is the Prince of Peace. And the war is screwing up everyone's life. Amen.

Christmas afternoon and evening are for playing games, visiting, shelling and eating nuts, sucking on hard candy, and gobbling down the apples and oranges Santa left in your stocking.

The evening radio was all music and static, maybe a little news. Eddie Cantor, Fibber McGee and Molly, Jack Benny, Bob Hope, and Red Skelton, my favorite programs were not on Christmas night. It was a peaceful time.

"Oh little town of Bethlehem, how still we see thee lie."

Someone knocked on the front door. Everyone dashed to open it, thinking Grandma and Grandpa finally arrived with their gifts. But it was Ellen Kramer with bad news. Rusty Schmidt's plane was shot down in the South Pacific. Rusty was class salutatorian and a hell of a basketball player. *"God rest ye merry gentlemen."*

The war ended August 15, 1945. Mrs. Myers, who owned the corner grocery store, cried as she told everybody the news. No more war next Christmas!

"Peace on earth. Good will toward men."

It doesn't have to be December, or even winter, to have the Christmas spirit. It's the thought, not the weather, that counts.

An older couple, probably in their eighties, sat at a small table in an outdoor café. It was late afternoon on what had been a rainy Florida day. The café was nearly empty. A guitarist was playing and singing music more suitable for the younger patrons who would arrive later in the evening.

A woman seated at a small table leaned toward her companion and said something. He reached into his pocket, said something to the woman and handed her a dollar bill. She smiled and turned again toward the singer. When the guitarist finished the piece, she walked to him, put the dollar bill in his tip jar and asked if he would play and sing *Country Roads*, a John Denver classic. He replied that he knew the music, but had never mastered the words.

"I'll give it a try," he said. The lady smiled and returned to her companion.

The entertainer hummed the tune, doing his best to honor the lady's request. Meanwhile, a young man from another small table strode toward the struggling singer with an open laptop that he placed in the singer's line of vision. Seeing the words to *Country Roads* on the computer screen, the singer stopped, began the song again and finished to the applause of everyone in the café.

The older couple rose, waved to the young man and put another dollar bill in the entertainer's tip jar as they left the café.

IX.

TWLIGHT ROMANCE

I am reminded of that old saying, "Snow on the roof doesn't mean there is no fire in the furnace." I haven't seen any storks around, but I know that love is alive and well in our twilight house.

How do I know? Well, we have some married couples here who hold hands. The elevator door opened on the first floor to reveal two unmarried residents from a higher floor caught kissing. Unmarried couples have traded two small apartments for one larger one. Second and even third marriages take place. Married couples renew their vows in our outdoor park area and on and on. Love, it seems, has no age limits.

I am going to inject a personal story here. My wife of sixty-four years died three years ago. I wrote about her death and my grief in *Musings of an Old Man* (2018). As I wrote then, "I walked without movement and talked without sound." I was convinced I would never recover from my grief. Then I met a widow, also a resident of my twilight house. We became friends and companions. Our relationship grew, and recently we were caught kissing when the elevator door opened on the first floor.

WAVES ON THE SHORE

My love flew away on silver wings
That only fly one way.
And I was left, alone and lost
To live each empty day.
The nights were lonely, sad and long.
I lay and cursed my plight.
Waited for the night to pass,
Prayed for morning light.
Then a sunbeam came to me,
Took me by the hand.
Led me to another place,
A place with sun and sand.
We stood upon the sand and watched
Each wave that reached the beach,
Splashed and rolled, stretching out
As far as it could reach.
We stood upon that sunny sand,
Waves splashing on that shore
And vowed while we were on life's beach
We would live and love once more.

Harry and Glenda are widowed and met at one of our bi-weekly happy hours here.

Happy hours serve free drinks and snacks and feature a two- or three-piece dance band. Harry and Glenda never miss a dance, well, maybe one or two to catch their breaths. They eat their meals together, take walks and spend free time together. Are they in love? I think so. Do they sleep together? Only they know.

Arlene and Carl had been happily married for sixty years when their happiness was threatened by Arlene's dementia. She was aware of her forgetfulness and began to avoid the socialization with the family and friends she and Carl had always enjoyed.

In addition, she neglected the housework their big house required and became fearful about cooking after she ruined several meals and burned a pan by forgetting to turn a burner off.

At the suggestion of their family physician Arlene underwent a four-hour examination by a neuropsychologist. The test results showed that while Arlene still had good upper-level reasoning and judgement skills, her short and long-term memory were significantly impaired. Arlene needed a smaller world than the one she was trying to manage. Since she and Carl were both in their eighties, the neuropsychologist recommended they investigate retirement communities. Carl finally became convinced that Arlene's problem could not be corrected and would likely be progressive.

With the help of a daughter they acted on the recommendation and found a continuing care community twelve miles from their house. They sold the house, donated most of their furniture to the Salvation Army and moved into a two-bedroom, two-bath apartment. Their meals, cleaning, maintenance, social activities and transportation were provided, although Carl kept their car.

Arlene did very well in her smaller world; Carl joined a card group and a billiards foursome. They no longer bickered and worried as they had in their single-family home. They were happily married again. I don't know if they were both sleeping in the same bedroom, but they were seen holding hands when they came into the dining room for breakfast.

★ ☆ ★

Henrietta (Henny) thought her life had come to an end when her husband, Bill, died. And, in a sense, it had. Her life with Bill as a sleeping partner was gone. The man she sat next to in church was gone. The father of her children gone, meals together, travels, tender moments, dancing partner, all gone. Bill wasn't coming back.

She remained in the house she and Bill had lived in for thirty years. But it seemed too big, too empty, too many memories.

Bill had done all the driving. Now the car was all hers and she hated driving it. Neighbors and friends seemed less interested in her company than they had been when Bill was alive. The children were mildly attentive, but they had their own lives to live, and they had very little in common with her. She was sad, lonely and depressed.

One day Henny received a call from Roberta, a former neighbor and good friend. Roberta had moved to a local retirement community after her husband died and called to see how Henny was getting along. Henny unloaded to Roberta and listened as Roberta related a similar tale of grief. She invited Henny to visit her and arranged a tour of the campus. Henny accepted, found an apartment she liked, sold her house and car and moved in. Her children were pleased to see their mother act and assisted with her move.

The transition wasn't easy, but Henny made friends, adjusted to community dining, volunteered for the library committee and was delighted to use the transportation services.

On Sundays she took the church bus to her church and rode with a man she knew from church. She and Bill had served on several church committees with him and his recently deceased wife.

Riding to church together grew to eating together, watching movies, Thursday evening beer and burgers at the beach, happy hour dances . . . and so on.

Two years later they were married in their twilight home chapel. Both their church minister and the twilight house chaplain officiated at the wedding. Roberta was her maid of honor, and all her children, with their children, attended and wished the newlyweds well.

A sad story is that of Ralph. He was widowed for five years before he found another love. Sarah, a widow, moved into an apartment down the hall. They developed a friendship that grew into a romance. Ralph gave Sarah an engagement ring on Valentine's Day.

They secured a two-bedroom, two-bath apartment on another floor and set a wedding date. Sarah suffered a stroke and died before they could be married.

It is not unusual for a single man or woman to find someone to share the end of life with, but their children don't always anticipate that happening. When it does, children may or may not be pleased. Take Charles as a for instance.

He had a large estate. He could afford a larger apartment and a more expensive car. But his children urged him to take a smaller apartment since he would be living alone. They also bought his new

Lincoln, too big for a man his age to drive, they argued, and bought him a used Chevrolet Cruze.

Then Charles met Betty and they became serious about each other. One of his children would have nothing to do with Betty, the other two treated her coolly. When Charles announced he had given Betty an engagement ring and planned a second marriage for both of them, all three children were irate. They cited his disloyalty to their mother, but Charles suspected, probably correctly, they were worried about sharing his estate.

On the other hand, I have met many kids of our residents and the residents of other twilight houses who seem delighted to have their parent in a loving relationship. Money may not be an issue in these cases.

Ira and Evelyn moved in as a married couple in their late eighties. Ira was in failing health, used a walker and had mild dementia. Evelyn was his caregiver, so they were permitted to have an apartment in independent living. After being residents for several months Ira fell, broke his hip and was admitted to the skilled-nursing unit, where he stayed for more than a month.

Evelyn visited him every day and was always with him for his physical therapy sessions. She also took her evening meal with him in his room. The staff observed she held his hand and hummed to him when he became upset, which was frequently. When the nurse came in at bedtime Evelyn kissed him and said, "Be a good boy."

Ira's hip healed, but his dementia worsened. Consequently, he was moved to an apartment in the assisted living unit. Evelyn could have remained in independent living and visited Ira often.

However, she chose to move also so she could be with him all the time. They are inseparable.

Most widows fare better as single persons than widowers do. Since the life expectancy of women is longer than that of men, our twilight house has women who have been widowed twice and even three times. They contradict the notion that women don't need a partner in their lives. Some do, but my experience is that men have more of a need.

Not all relationships are romantic. Many simply provide companionship. A widower in a relationship with a widow told me their romance had never progressed beyond holding hands. And that was fine for both.

Marjory lost her husband to cancer one month after they moved in. Within months she had developed a relationship with Tim, a victim of Parkinson's disease with serious mobility problems. When he required a wheelchair, she pushed it. She loaded his walker and drove him to his appointments, and she assisted him in the dining room when he needed assistance. It was a desirable relationship for both. He needed care, and she needed someone to care for. But more than that, they were truly fond of each other. When Tim died, Marjory moved to a twilight house in a city nearer her children.

★ ☆ ★

As you can see, romance thrives in twilight houses. Whether women or men initiate companionships more is not important. Whether relationships include sexual activity is also not important. It is important that many people find a person to share the remainder of their lives with.

I have written in *Musings of an Old Man* of the debilitating grief that follows the loss of a spouse. I know I am not alone in finding solace and renewal with another companion, partner, lady friend, boyfriend, lover . . . whatever. Married people rarely die together. One is most often left to watch another sunset. Those who are fortunate find someone to watch another sunset with. It's easier to find such a person in a twilight house than it is in a single-family home or living with children. Old people need romance too.

THE CLOVER AND THE KEY

I held my sweet Mary 'till the moment she died.
She had given me sunshine, blue skies and pride.
But then came the dark clouds, the thunder and rain,
I was glad when it ended. God relieved her of pain.
I thought when she died my life was over.
But God found and sent me a four-leaf clover.
A clover named Rose came into my life.
She had some years before been another man's wife.
Now a widow, she was wary of me.
But God in His kindness sent her a key,
The key to my lonely, old heart.
It beat once again, and got her heart to start.
So now we're together, Rosie and I,
Living with sunshine and mostly blue sky.
I can't forget Mary, would not if I could.
But life with Rosie is pretty darn good.
I know she thinks often of her other life,
The years she spent as another man's wife.
And I still cherish Mary, the life we two had.

We walked hand in hand through the good and the bad.
But we're alive again, Rosie and me:
And grateful to God for that clover and key.

I end this chapter on a light note with the following vignette.

Arthur Samuelson was one of the boys who sat at the widowers' table in the dining room at *Pleasant Acres*. It was one of those names given to homes for old folks to make them sound appealing. It had been renamed each time the occupancy rate dropped and marketing needed an excuse for poor sales. Its history included names of *Rolling Meadows, Restful Arms, Peaceful Pasture and Happy Hallways.* They all seemed to work until a new home for old folks sprouted with a name that fetched potential buy-ins on the waiting list of whatever Pleasant Acres was called at the time.

Arthur had been a resident through two name changes and sometimes gave one of the former names when asked where he lived. It didn't much matter because the name would soon be changed anyway, unlike the widowers' table. That name never changed even when one of the six old men who sat there every meal died and a newcomer to Pleasant Acres, or whatever it was called, took his place.

Arthur and his wife, Sally, moved into Pleasant Acres when it was Peaceful Pasture. He had just turned eighty, and Sally was seventy-eight. They had been married fifty years, high school sweethearts.

Sally had been kissed by two boys, one after sophomore prom and one after junior prom. Arthur's first kiss was after senior prom when he saw Sally puckered up and figured out what she had in mind.

Obviously, Sally was more experienced than Arthur, so both agreed romantic decisions would be better left to Sally. She decided on a temperate, sensible honeymoon, and Arthur agreed. She decided on two children and he went along. Eventually she stopped making decisions, and Arthur took up woodworking and ball games with the kids.

They moved to *Peaceful Pasture* because of Sally's chronic fatigue. Doctors discovered she had a genetic heart defect that could not be helped by surgery or any other "tool they had in their toolbox," as Arthur explained it. She was given some medications, advised to rest as much as possible and to avoid stress. Her mother and sister died young of the same heart condition, and she expected an abbreviated life expectancy as well. She was correct.

To follow doctors' orders, prepare Arthur for her demise and to secure his well-being after, she decided they should move to Peaceful Pasture. He agreed. She was perceptive, and for the first time in her life discovered that unmarried older couples frolicked together and who knew what else. There were also second, and even third marriages. One couple was caught kissing in the elevator when the door opened on the first floor. All those goings-on prompted her to decide she and Arthur should "try it once more." They did and although her heart beat faster it didn't stop. So they tried it every Saturday night.

Sally also took note of the widowers' table and, had there been a waiting list, would have signed Arthur up for it—single men only!

After three happy, stress-free years Sally died at Pleasant Acres in the skilled nursing unit, but not before she gave Arthur his instructions. He was to mind their children, who were "good kids" and then, to the surprise of Arthur and herself she said, "And when I'm gone, find a nice lady to look after you. You need someone to make decisions for you, Arthur, someone kind and thoughtful. I won't mind a bit. Sit with the other men until she comes along. You are a good man, Arthur, you'll see. I won't mind a bit." Arthur was too astonished to protest.

After Sally's death, Arthur took Billy Hastock's chair at the widowers' table. Billy was snatched away by Harley Lindstrom's wife after Harley died.

"No sense living alone if you don't have to," Billy explained.

Nobody talked much at the widowers' table, and women intuitively knew better than to take a seat there. If a lady wanted to strike up a conversation or walk to the bingo room or a movie with one of the men there, she waited at the mailboxes where everyone went after dinner to collect their postage. She waited for the man of her choice to appear. Then she employed the old hanky trick, using a piece of mail instead of a hanky.

"Oh, my. How clumsy of me. Are you going to the movie tonight? May I tag along?"

Arthur seemed not to notice how men at the widowers' table came and went. He missed Sally something awful, and their kids were always busy or working or out of town on vacations. He was a lonely man. When he tried joining in the activities provided, he felt out of place, except in the woodworking shop, which became his daily and evening refuge.

Marjorie, "just call me Marge," moved into Pleasant Acres on a Wednesday. She had been widowed eight years and had just left a boyfriend at Holiday Homestead. He was too damn controlling. She couldn't shake him without a scene, so she moved—on Wednesday.

Marjorie was no novice. She spotted the widowers' table on Thursday, sized up Arthur on Friday, and made her move on Saturday. Cully Johnson was late getting to his chair next to Arthur, and Marjorie took it, requiring Cully to sit at the bridge ladies table where he was relegated to playing dummy for the entire meal.

Marjorie explained to the boys that she was new to Pleasant Acres, and would they tell her, "how this lovely place worked." She had been a high school English teacher and, "Have you all read *Catcher in the Rye?*"

Before dessert Marjorie complained of feeling faint, asking Arthur if he minded seeing her to her apartment. Arthur said he had a table reserved in the woodworking shop, but he would help her first. The bridge ladies and Cully watched them leave the dining room arm in arm. Cully returned to his chair.

As they reached her apartment, Marjorie experienced a fainting spell and stumbled at her door. Arthur caught her, and not knowing what came over him, he kissed her forehead. Marjorie knew by the way he held her and clumsily kissed her that Arthur had a lot to learn, but she was a good teacher. And Arthur recalled Sally's words, "I won't mind a bit."

And he really didn't have a table reserved at the woodworking shop anyway.

X.

TWILIGHT SUNSET

Death is no stranger to residents of a twilight house. Most people who move from single-family living to a CCRC have experienced a cognitive or physical change that requires living with assistance. In many cases one spouse develops a health problem that demands a different lifestyle for both. I could no longer provide for my wife and me in our single-family home when her health deteriorated. I write about that in detail in *Life After Eighty* (2016).

Many others move here after a spouse has died and they can no longer, or don't want to, live alone. They too are near or past their life-expectancies and are likely to have health problems. Healthy, young people don't take up residence in a twilight house.

So both the age and the health of twilight house residents makes death an expected event.

I am reminded here of a poem by Percy Shelley (1792 – 1822).

OZYMANDIAS

. . . Two vast and trunkless legs of stone
Stand in the desert. Near them, on the sand,
Half sunk, a shattered visage lies. . .
And on the pedestal these words appear;
'My name is Ozymandias, King of Kings;
Look on my works, ye mighty, and despair.'
Nothing beside remains. Round the decay
Of that colossal wreck, boundless and bare
The loan and level sands stretch far away.

Nobody and nothing last forever. That's as true for the powerful as for those of us with less spectacular lives. The floor I live on has twelve apartments. In the almost six years I have lived here every apartment has a new occupant or occupants because of deaths. These apartments are in the *independent-living* units. Those in *assisted-living* and *memory-care* units have an even greater turnover rate.

Most of our residents die in the *skilled-nursing* unit. Often, they move from their apartments after a stay in a hospital. Few die in the apartments they moved into. Medicare doesn't pay for patients in skilled nursing without a three-day stay in a hospital. Many of those who are diagnosed as terminal with a short time to live engage hospice care for their final weeks or months. My experience with hospice care and the experiences of others I know warrant high praise for hospice care.

So, all of this begs the question: How do those of us still living in the sunshine maintain the good morale we have while the sun is setting on so many of our neighbors? I think part of the answer lies in the growing acceptance of death as we grow older. We no longer fear death as we once did, perhaps because we have less to lose. Perhaps because loss is already such a part of our lives. Perhaps because we believe in a heavenly reward. Perhaps because we are tired of living with infirmities and fragility. Perhaps because we have simply accepted the inevitability of death.

Nonetheless, most of us are happy, active and in good spirits more than we are not. We do what we can to stay in the sunshine of our lives even as we say goodbye to those upon whom the sun has set.

Our twilight house has two chapels and two chaplains. When my wife died, one of our chaplains was by my side, as were our children. Our chaplains are busy before, during and after our deaths. Perhaps their accessibility and the comfort they give help in our acceptance of death. They have seen a lot of it and know the right things to say, whether or not we are believers. We are all believers in death and the crashing grief it brings to those close to the deceased.

The chapels themselves bring comfort. They are an integral part of the place we have come to call home. They and our chaplains are always available to family of anyone who lives or lived here. Memorial services in our chapels are well-attended by those of us for whom the sun has not yet set.

I end this chapter, and this book, with two poetic references. One, the English poet, William Wordsworth (1770 – 1850) wrote in "Ode: Intimation of Immortality:"

> *Our birth is but a sleep and a forgetting;*
> *The soul that rises with us, our life's star,*
> *Hath had elsewhere its setting*
> *And cometh from afar;*
> *Not in entire forgetfulness,*
> *And not in utter nakedness,*
> *But trailing clouds of glory do we come*
> *From God who is our home.*

And Henry Van Dyke (1852 –1933) wrote in "Gone from My Sight:"

> *I am standing upon the seashore.*
> *A ship at my side, spreads her white sails*
> *To the moving breeze*
> *And starts for the blue ocean . . .*
> *Then someone at my side says, "There, she is gone" . . .*
> *And, just at the moment when someone says,*
> *"There, she is gone." There are other eyes*
> *Watching her coming, and other voices*
> *Ready to take up the glad shout, "Her she comes!"*
> *And, that is dying.*

Perhaps when we die we return to the place and state we were in before we were born, as Wordsworth implied. Perhaps not. Many still believe in a heaven for the good and a hell for the bad.

Some believe, as Van Dyke proposes, that death is a journey to another shore and whatever and whoever is on that shore.

Our differing beliefs suggest some degree of uncertainty within our population. But we all agree that the sunshine we now enjoy will be followed by a sunset.

TIME

> *I pass by the memorial benches lining Ware's Creek*
> *And only one has a name of someone I remember.*
> *The names on the other benches are unknown to me.*
> *Someday, someone may buy and put my name on a bench.*
> *For a time, people will pass and say, "Yes, I knew him well."*
> *But time will also pass, and passersby will say,*
> *"I wonder who he was, that name on the bench."*

ACKNOWLEDGMENTS

This book is a collection of the poetry, essays and commentary I wrote for the enjoyment of the residents of Westminster Point Pleasant, a continuing care retirement community in Bradenton, Florida. I must acknowledge those resident readers for providing me the material, encouragement and inspiration for my writings.

I am also indebted to residents of other retirement communities who read what I wrote and expressed their approval. Some younger readers acted as critics for me as well. They all had some familiarity with Twilight Houses.

Carole Sanders, former editor of our community newspaper, the *ECHO,* and present editor of the *WRITER'S QUARTERLY,* has for years been my first reader, my kindest critic and my editor. She was never shy about saying, "You can do better than this." She guided the organization and production of *Tales* as if it were her own.

My friends of many years, Jo and Roy Williams, now residents of a neighboring retirement community, read pre-edited copy and offered their comments and insights.

Finally, I must give thanks to John Koehler and his staff at Koehler Books, a publishing company that has been a delight to work with for this book and the three others we published together.

CPSIA information can be obtained
at www.ICGtesting.com
Printed in the USA
LVHW050009071020
668069LV00006B/577